Praise for *Say It Out Loud*

Always being the 'good girl,' pleasing others, and internalizing your feelings is self-destructive. Our childhood is stored in our body, and if we do not heal our wounds someday, the body will present its bill. Roberta Dolan had the courage to transform and heal herself. The techniques she utilized to do so and the changes she made can benefit all those who have ever been abused, physically or psychologically. I strongly recommend reading this book to help you to release whatever pain exists within you and to restore your own life and body. It is never too late to leave the past behind and begin anew, as Roberta did.

—**Bernie Siegel**, MD, author of *365 Prescriptions for the Soul* and *101 Exercises for the Soul*

Roberta Dolan has found the courage to tell the story of her horrific sexual abuse in a book with the smart title *Say It Out Loud*. At least as much effort is spent on guiding others through the process, step by step, for which she is eminently qualified, not only as a survivor, but as a counselor with a master's degree. But it is her own story that is the most compelling as she mines the darkest corners of her soul with honesty and integrity. By nurturing the healing process of others along the way, she heals herself. And that is contagious. I recommend her book to survivors at all stages of healing and to those who love and support survivors."

—**Trish Kinney**, author of *Silver Platter Girl*

In *Say It Out Loud*, Roberta Dolan has unpacked the vicissitudes of her own personal healing journey in a way that informs, supports, encourages, and inspires others who have been sexually abused and those who love them. Practical in its structure, her sensitivity and compassion flow from each paragraph. Prescriptive but not preachy, there is an intelligent, uplifting, kind, and gentle quality about *Say It Out Loud* which is unique among books of this genre and which I believe makes it accessible to readers at any point of their own journey."

—**Catherine McCall LMFT**, author of *When the Piano Stops* and *Never Tell: A True Story of Overcoming a Terrifying Childhood*

In *Say It Out Loud*, Roberta Dolan courageously attacks the major obstacles to preventing sexual assault—secrecy and silence. Fearless and determined, Dolan holds nothing back as she charges full force—revealing personal experience through raw and powerful journal entries, and exposing and coping with the psychological damage caused by sexual assault. As victim, teacher, counselor, wife, and mother, Dolan presents insight to all sides of the healing journey. More than an affirmation of inspiration, *Say It Out Loud* serves as a practical guide of easy-to-follow strategies. Survivors will know they're not alone, and they'll come to realize the possibility of restoring a joyful life. For loved ones, counselors and therapists, *Say It Out Loud* should be required reading.

—**Kathy Marcantonio**, former counselor and community
education volunteer of Connecticut Sexual Assault
Crisis Services, Inc. (ConnSACS) Board of Directors

Say It Out Loud by Roberta Dolan is an intimate and courageous account of the steps that must be taken to recover from predatory sexual abuse. Dolan shares her healing process by walking the reader through her agony and into her eventual experience of joy. The complexities and beauty of the human heart are exposed in a frightened child now adult, who, because of the care of a therapist and a loving husband, can finally be free.

—**Gwen Plano**, author of *Letting Go Into Perfect Love*

Roberta Dolan has singlehandedly, with honesty and love, provided us with not only a moving account of her experience but a practical guide for those recovering from childhood sexual abuse. Without hesitation, I recommend this book to those dealing with the lingering effects of childhood sexual abuse, to those family members and friends who support a survivor, and to those who work with survivors and their families. Dolan has changed, and will continue to change, lives.

—**Sharon D. Chappelle, PhD**

Say It
Out Loud

Say It
Out Loud

REVEALING *and* HEALING *the*
SCARS *of* SEXUAL ABUSE

Roberta Dolan

SHE WRITES PRESS

Published 2014
Printed in the United States of America
ISBN: 978-1-938314-99-5
Library of Congress Control Number: 2014936062

For information, address:
She Writes Press
1563 Solano Ave #546
Berkeley, CA 94707

Dedication

December 4, 2005

Tim was by my side, in touch with my needs, incredible as always. Someday, somewhere, he has to get recognized for what h. has so selflessly done.

That *someday* is today as I dedicate this book to my husband, Tim Dolan. *Selfless* describes perfectly his involvement in my healing journey. When he is asked how he did it, his response is always the same: "Did what? I didn't do anything. I just loved her."

Loving me, for Tim, meant anticipating my needs by watching and listening to my actions, my tone, and sometimes my silence. When I needed to be nudged, he nudged. When I needed to be left in silence, he let me be. When I needed to be held, he held me, and when I needed to be safe, he kept me safe. In my darkest moments, when I chose to isolate myself, I knew deep in my heart I was not alone—he would not let me slip away.

Tim was my voice with our children and our friends, letting others know what I needed and showing them the way to support me by his example.

He never tired of reassuring me that I was going to be okay, we were going to make it through this, and I was not alone. He willingly participated in whatever strategy was necessary to get me to the next phase of my journey and never tried to control my path. When he didn't know what to do, he asked.

Tim believed me, and believed *in* me, from the first day I uttered the words "I think my father abused me." His response that day changed my life. By not doubting me, and by offering immediate support, he gave me the courage to take the crucial steps of seeking a therapist and facing my demons.

Tim selflessly put his life aside for six years to help me heal. I would need a thousand lifetimes to "just love him" the way he loved me. For now, I dedicate this book, and my life, to loving him.

Contents

Part I: Preparing for the Journey

Part II: Tools for the Journey

Part III: Living the Journey

Part IV: Life

Foreword

When Roberta told me she was writing a book about her sexual abuse and her desire to encourage other abuse victims to "say it out loud" and begin their healing process, I was not surprised.

I *was* surprised to learn she had done such meticulous journaling after her heart-wrenching treatment sessions. That allowed her to write this accurate account of her fears, anger, pain, trepidation, and, finally, "freedom" from her past.

My role in Roberta's healing was to be present and to assure her that she was not alone on this journey—I would be there for her and with her. Her role was to uncover and liberate herself from the horrific parts of her past. She accomplished this goal after six long years, one treatment session at a time.

Roberta did a truly wonderful job, which this book reveals. I believe she offers many ideas and strategies that can assist, encourage, and support sexual abuse victims during their own journey. If any victim out there wishes to begin the healing process, please start by reading *Say It Out Loud: Revealing and Healing the Scars of Sexual Abuse*.

Respectfully,
Dellene Watt Quintiliani
Licensed Clinical Social Worker

Prologue

A View from the Inside: October 24, 2001

What did I do? I know I didn't yell. I know I retracted into myself. I know I froze. I started talking about it—about lying on my stomach. Before long my eyes were closed, my fists clenched. I was there again, experiencing the whole thing. I made my hands hurt so I wouldn't feel the pain, I made loud noises in my head to block it out. When it was over my body relaxed, then I got tense again. My hands were down gripping the sides of the bed, trying to keep my legs together, but he forced them open. I created my own pain—made loud noises in my head—then it's over and I relax. I roll on my side in a tight fetal position and sob, but silently. I sob until I can't breathe—tucked in a ball, against the wall, clutching my teddy bear.

I am Roberta Ann Dolan, born on September 2, 1952 to Rune and Clara Frisk. I have one sister, two years older than I am. We shared our single-family home in Connecticut with my maternal grandfather. Rune, an alcoholic, died of cancer in 1989. Clara remained in the same house by herself.

Part I:
Preparing for the Journey

"Preparing for the Journey" introduces you to my personal healing journey and to the essential parameters and relationships necessary for beginning a healing journey of your own.

1
Setting the Stage

A View from the Outside

Seat yourself on a lawn chair across the street, and I will paint a picture for you.

It's a modest, dark-gray house on a corner lot in a working-class community. A lush green lawn and colorful flower beds surround the house. Red and white geraniums and petunias fill the freshly painted window boxes. Most days, a line of crisp, clean laundry stretches across the yard.

Step into the kitchen. You're greeted by the delicate aroma of something cooking or baking. The entire house sparkles, and nothing is out of place.

Rune's basement work area is much the same. Each tool hangs in its assigned spot, and the floor is swept clean. A stool, a clean ashtray, and a pack of Camel nonfilters sit by the workbench. The beer is kept out of sight under the stairwell: Ruppert Knickerbocker bottles, room temperature, just the way he likes them.

Before Clara retires for the night, she sets the table for breakfast and Rune prepares a pot of coffee for the next day. In the morning, he goes off to his job as a tool-and-die designer in a pressed shirt, tie, and jacket. His appearance is as immaculate as the home he steps out of. The girls go off to school dressed in the same pristine style. Clara remains home to clean, garden, do laundry, iron, and prepare lunch and dinner for her family. She is admired in the community as a Scout leader and PTA mom, both coveted roles.

A typical Saturday might include a family picnic, a boat ride, or a hike through the woods. Sundays are ritualistic. Rune drives his wife and daughters to church. He is a Methodist, and she is a devout Catholic. He drops them off and is waiting for them when Mass ends. Afterward, Clara prepares a special Sunday dinner while Rune takes the girls to visit his parents. A leisurely afternoon follows. The weekend culminates with the family sitting in front of their small black-and-white television, watching *The Ed Sullivan Show*.

My abuse began when I was three or four years old and continued through my early teens. My cries for help went unanswered. The purpose of my writing is not to document these horrific memories but to share the process that brought me to life—the life I now have.

From Little Girl to Woman

Before I begin to share that process, it is necessary to convey a bit of background, a closer look into the personality of the little girl, from child to woman. Her appearance: a good girl, one who liked to please, always willing to help. Her reality: a fragile child, seeking approval, needing to be seen, never feeling good enough. Someone spending a lifetime trying to be "the good daughter."

As a child, eager to do the right thing. As a teen, Clara's confidant during the worst years of Rune's alcoholism. As an adult, taking care of Clara's needs and striving to gain her attention and approval. All the while never feeling as smart, good, pretty, or well liked as her peers.

I secretly doubted most of my decisions and always fell short of feeling accomplished or whole. However, my internal struggles did not prevent me from achieving a successful career; rather, they may have increased my drive to please. Thirty-three years as a special-education teacher, Teacher of the Year for my school district, and assistant to the principal of an urban elementary school were just some of my professional accomplishments.

My first marriage, to my high school sweetheart, ended in divorce. Soon thereafter, I met the man who became my best friend and partner for life. We built our home, a geodesic dome, and were married in it in 1982. Tim and I were blessed with two beautiful children of our own and a daughter from his first marriage. As a family, we were involved in our church, our school, and the normal activities that come with raising children. I gave the children's sermon at our church and directed the Cherub Choir. I served as a member and president of the PTO at our children's school.

It all looked wonderful, and for the most part, it *was*. I loved my role as educator, wife, and mother. I just didn't love myself. There was something wrong with me, but I didn't know what it was.

The Little Girl with the Big Secret

I have no memory of ever telling anyone what was happening to me. I do remember I often cried at night, calling, "Mom, Mommy, Mom, Mommy." Clara either did not answer those cries or silenced them by telling me to be quiet and go to sleep. I also remember frequent nightmares and no one coming to calm my fears. I believe the little girl learned early on that the abuse was a secret never to be shared. If Mommy didn't respond to my cries for help, who would? If Mommy didn't tell anyone, how could I? If the two people I was supposed to trust the most were hurting me, then whom could I tell? Maybe I deserved this terror; maybe I had done something wrong and wasn't worth saving.

It was that terrified little girl who held the secret deep inside for many years. Then, sometime in my thirties, I had a dream. I was a teenager, sitting on Rune's lap, and he was kissing me. In the dream, Clara blamed me for the encounter. As I drove to work the next morning, I could barely function. I experienced intense anxiety. I asked our school social worker if she had any knowledge of dream analysis. Her limited response allowed me to dismiss my dream as nothing more than a meaningless event—and I didn't want it to be anything more.

A few years later, I remembered a real-life scene in my family's living room: I was eight years old. Rune was in his chair, watching television, when I went over to say good night. He grabbed my hand, forced it onto his crotch, and started kissing me in a way that made me feel sick. Clara came to the doorway and yelled, "Rune, what are you doing?" I ran to my room, frightened, confused, and alone.

Even though I knew this incident was real, my reaction was to minimize it. After all, he was drunk and Clara never did anything about it, so how bad could it have been? But as hard as I tried to dismiss the thoughts, both the dream and the memory burned inside me like an ember that could not be extinguished. It was only a matter of time.

The Beginning

It was March 2000. Our friend Nancy cared for the children, and Tim and I went away for the weekend. He and I were so close and happy. We were best friends and prided ourselves on our openness as a couple. We had no doubt about the love we shared. So what was wrong? A familiar conversation began.

Tim expressed again that he sensed something missing, that there was a part of me he did not have. In our most intimate moments, when expressions of love should have had no boundaries, I held back. Why? What was in the way? My usual response: "I don't know."

What made this day different, we'll never know. As easily as "I don't know" had come from my lips so many times in the past, I responded, "I think I know. I think my father abused me when I was young."

I shared with Tim the dream and the only memory that had shown its ugly face to me. We talked for a while. The dream and the memory were real, but I remained doubtful, needing to hold on to the hope that they were insignificant. But now that the tiny ember had been given a breath of air, it burned hotter and could no longer be ignored.

My thoughts kept returning to the memory. I was distracted and tense. By December, Tim convinced me I needed to share these thoughts with a professional. With great trepidation, I made the phone call that would change my life.

The First Step of the Journey

On January 3, 2001, I took the biggest step of my life: I walked into the office of Dellene, the woman who would be my therapist for the next six years. With my outfit freshly ironed, hair combed, and lips glossed, I projected an image of control as I extended my hand to greet her. Only my pounding heart told the true story. After a few preliminary questions, she asked, "So, what brought you here tonight?"

Without hesitation, I replied, "I think my father was sexually inappropriate with me as a child." I shared with her my one clear memory, the living room scene that had emerged a few years earlier. I exuded an air of nonchalance, making it clear that Rune had been an alcoholic—my effort to minimize what had happened. Although I wasn't sure there was more to talk about, I felt safe enough to make a second appointment before leaving. The drive home from that first session is as vivid in my mind today as it was the day it occurred. All the way home, I laughed and I cried, saying over and over, "I did it. I told someone. I said it out loud!"

Once you say it out loud, you can't take it back. It is out. The secret is no longer locked inside. The burning ember is ignited. Hard work, tears, expressing the anger, and acceptance are the only means to extinguish the raging fire. In the chapters to follow, I will share the experiences and strategies that led me from that first session, in 2001, to the present.

Each person's story of sexual abuse is different, and each needs to follow his or her own path to healing. Sadly, too few succeed. I am living proof that one can face demons, relive the hell, and in the end say, "I am healed. I am whole." No one deserves to live in the darkness abuse creates, and no one has to accept the life of a victim. You *can* choose to release yourself from that dark chamber. You *can* do it, you *are* worth it, and you are *not* alone! The strategies within this book are the tools you will need. My purpose for exposing my story is to take the shame out of being sexually abused and lead the way for others on their journey to becoming whole.

2
Ground Rules

There are no right or wrong strategies or techniques to use as you work through the stages of healing. From experience, I suggest setting parameters for approaching any strategy. The four essential ground rules to my well-being were: maintain safety, honor feelings, be honest, and regulate control.

First, and most important, be safe within your environment and safe from within. Whether the situation involves expressing rage, needing to be alone, taking medication, releasing the pain, or reliving memories, you must keep yourself safe. Being safe may mean sharing thoughts with someone close to you, asking that person to remain aware of where you are physically and emotionally. As much as you desire to isolate yourself, experiencing the stages of healing alone is not the safest plan. If you compromise your safety, you'll compromise your goal to heal. There were many times during my healing process when I needed to be alone. Telling someone my destination and having a cell phone with me simultaneously allowed me the space I needed and gave me a safety net.

Second, be aware of what feels right for you, and honor those feelings. This is not the time to be the pleaser, the gracious person who doesn't want to offend anyone. This is about you and your healing process. Others can and will help you, but no one else knows what feels right for you except you. Some of the strategies I write about will feel comfortable and will even be approaches you've already tried. Others may be new, but you will be willing to try them. Other strategies I share will feel too foreign, uncomfortable, or irritating, like a scratchy sweater—things you would never consider doing. Honor your intuition. Just keep in mind that any strategy, whether it is right or wrong for you, can spark new ideas. You will read in chapter 9, "Anger," about a time when I did not honor my feelings and instead tried a strategy outside of my comfort zone that resulted only in greater frustration. The positive side is that the failed attempt helped me to understand my own needs and develop strategies that worked for me.

Third, be honest with others, but, more important, be honest with yourself. I spent more than forty years pretending I had a near-perfect life. Well, life isn't perfect while you're doing the work to heal. There will be days when you won't want to talk with anyone, days when going to the grocery store will become an unbearable task, weekends when the thought of socializing will evoke anxiety. If the task or event is not essential, say no. Limit your social plans if you aren't up to it. Put chores off a day or two until you can handle them. Don't accept a phone call if you're not up to talking.

It is okay to not be okay! Give yourself permission. Healing is a long process and a time when you won't have the energy to keep up the appearance that you're "fine." This is not to say you should tell everyone your life story; there are places and times when it is most appropriate to politely say you are fine. Most times, you will recognize the difference. For example, if you are talking with a casual acquaintance or are walking into an important meeting and don't want to raise your level of anxiety, you are likely to respond, "I'm fine." If you aren't sure of what to say, it's also best to say you are fine. You can always revisit a conversation with someone if you decide you want to share more information. However, right from the start of your healing process, your therapist, significant other, and closest friends need to know the truth. They can't help you if they don't know what you're feeling, and you cannot share with them what you need unless you're honest with yourself. In my therapist's words, "There are no right or wrong feelings. They are just your feelings." Be honest with yourself and those helping you. There's no room for pretending once you have committed to healing.

Finally, know when to retain control and when to relinquish it to others. Any form of abuse strips a victim of control. The need to be in control lingers for survivors long after the abuse has ended. Maintaining control is an asset when it permits you to make healthy choices. It becomes a liability when the need for control prevents you from accepting help from others. Regulating control is the key. This issue of control is so important that chapter 7 is devoted to it.

Summary

The goal of a healing journey is to improve your life. Applying a few ground rules as you implement strategies will help you achieve that goal without causing further damage. By maintaining safety, honoring feelings, being honest, and regulating control, you'll be on your way to a safe healing journey.

3
Relationships

There is no hope of joy except in human relations.
—Antoine de Saint-Exupéry

Once someone has been sexually abused, one time or repeatedly—as a child, a teen, or an adult—their ability to form and maintain relationships changes. That person has a strong need to be in control and to feel physically and emotionally protected. That sense of protection is accomplished by creating an invisible barrier. For some, no one is allowed to break that barrier; for others, a loved one may get close, but there's still a veil of separation. A fear looms—the fear of being vulnerable again. *Dare I let anyone break the shell of this well-protected body?*

Depression, anxiety, and anger are all physically palpable scars of abuse. Vulnerability is subtle, an internal scar that must be addressed if the healing journey is to be complete. In many entries in my journals, I describe feeling isolated and alone, not wanting to let anyone in. It is a frightening place to be, and a mindset that will not promote healing. I've chosen the following journal entry to share because it illustrates the contradiction that I was keeping myself in isolation and yet sad that I felt alone.

July 11, 2001

I feel alone. But it is my own fault. It's because I won't let anyone in. I feel isolated and trapped in my thoughts. I don't want to think in the present—I want to stay isolated and emotionally empty.

Facing demons is not a task anyone should tackle alone. Relationships provide the external support and nurturing necessary to move forward. Once the hard work is done and you are well on your way to healing, you should not tackle life alone, either. We all need to connect with other human beings, to love and feel loved. It's our nature.

So how do you crack that exterior shell and let others in? In this chapter, I will discuss relationships and share strategies for connecting with others who will help you on your journey and disconnecting from those who will prevent you from healing.

Connecting

Family, friends, colleagues, and acquaintances exist on some level in everyone's life. The goal is to develop healthy relationships with everyone in your circle, but that can happen only in small stages. I will discuss the importance of trust and open communication and offer strategies for establishing these essential relationship elements through three examples, one involving a therapist, one a partner, and one a friend. Once you have broken the barrier and are ready, the breadth of your relationships will grow naturally.

Connecting with a Therapist

If you are committed to healing, the first connection you'll need to make is with a therapist, but finding the right one can be daunting. A primary care physician, clergy member, or local crisis hotline can help you find a reputable therapist in your area.

While choosing a therapist, you'll want to address several important considerations. The first is gender. (I, for one, knew I would only feel comfortable talking to a female therapist.) Next, once you've decided on a therapist to contact, ask a few housekeeping questions, either by requesting a phone consultation or at your first appointment:

- How much do you charge?
- What insurance do you accept?
- What are your areas of expertise?
- How long have you been in practice?
- What's your appointment cancellation policy?
- What if I have a crisis on the weekend or a holiday?

If you aren't comfortable with the first therapist's answers, you should consider interviewing another candidate. You do not want to start therapy with someone you can't afford or someone who's never worked with sexual abuse survivors. The conditions need to be right for therapy to be successful.

I was fortunate to find the right person, but not because I was prepared with questions. Although I was ready to seek the help of a therapist, I was not yet ready to admit why I needed therapy. When I asked my nurse practitioner for a recommendation, I stated that I had issues as an adult child of an alcoholic. She gave me the name of a therapist who works with families of alcoholics. When I called for the appointment, the secretary informed me that the person did not participate in my insurance and suggested the name of another therapist who did. Based on my need for insurance coverage, I said fine and booked an appointment. As I learned a few sessions later, my therapist's expertise involved working with victims of sexual abuse.

In my situation, finding the right therapist was due to luck—or, as I prefer to think, divine intervention. However, I recommend making an informed choice rather than leaving it to chance.

If you are satisfied with the prospective therapist's answers to your questions, the next important criterion for making a connection is whether the therapist's personal traits and therapeutic style are a good match for you. You will know this only after a few visits. If you aren't comfortable with the person for any reason, it is imperative that you look for someone new. It is not uncommon to try out two or three therapists before finding the one who is right. This may be the most important decision you make on your healing journey.

I left my first visit with my therapist, Dellene, with a good impression, but I did not yet fully trust her or know the extent to which I would depend on her. My trust grew with time. I wrote the following journal entry two and a half months into therapy, after sharing with Dellene the message I got from my parents: I was not worth it—not worth taking care of, protecting, loving.

March 27, 2001

Dellene said it was the message but not the reality. It is hard to stop crying. It is the first time I really exposed myself to Dellene. When I left I hugged her. I must feel so safe with her.

Without feeling safe, I'd not have been able to continue exposing the darkness of my past. Dellene and I met once a week for six years and then as needed. She gave me a hotline number to call whenever I needed her. During some of my most desperate times, she met me at the center for unscheduled visits at night or on weekends. Dellene was committed to my healing, she cared about me, she was non-judgmental, and she let me be in control—all qualities I needed to establish a trusting relationship.

Dellene's allowing me to be in control was the most significant component of my progress, and a style not all therapists share. Each time I walked into her office, she let me steer the conversation. She may have guided me with questions once I started, but I was always in control of what we discussed. During a session one month into my therapy, I brought up a topic that troubled me. I perceived some of my characteristics as a child as "bad." The following was Dellene's response.

February 7, 2001

It was survival. It was normal, not bad. She said I did not feel protected—no, I was not protected by the two people who were supposed to protect me—and then she said "your father and mother."

It was the first time I had a glimpse of my mother's involvement in my abuse. I froze at the thought, not wanting to go there. We discussed that I wasn't ready to handle my mother. It took months for me to acknowledge Clara's choice to not protect me, and years for my memories of her abuse to surface. Dellene suspected Clara's involvement in my abuse not more than a month into my therapy. If she had forced the conversation in 2001, I suspect I would have denied it and struggled internally with the thought. At the time, I could barely maintain emotional stability in dealing with Rune's abuse. Talking about Clara could have sent me back into complete denial or, at the least, impeded my progress. But because Dellene's style was to let the client be in control, I felt safe and trusted her on my journey.

If your therapist drives the conversation and addresses issues you aren't ready to confront, you do not have to walk out the door. Explain your need for control and ask if the therapist is willing to work at your pace. If, after a few sessions, the agenda still seems to be the therapist's and not your own, then I suggest you explain that this arrangement isn't working for you and that you will seek the help of another therapist. But do not give up! You must follow through and find a therapist who is the right fit.

The obvious reason for needing trust in a therapist-client relationship is that you'll be sharing your most private, frightening, and fragile thoughts with this person. The benefit is that trust will allow you to shed inhibitions, something that's necessary in the process of healing. As you address the emotions of abuse, you'll most likely use strong language and exhibit behaviors that are extreme. I sobbed, with my nose running, for entire sessions; I pounded my fists; like a stubborn child, I refused to talk; I shared graphic nightmares, memories, and thoughts I would not tell another soul. When you are dealing with the filth, pain, and anger of sexual abuse, you must be able to express yourself in any way that results in your feeling cleansed. There is no room for inhibitions or embarrassment. That requires trust.

Establishing trust takes time, but you'll sense it is building based on how you feel before, during, and after your sessions. Before my sessions, I did not fear my therapist's questions or worry about her pushing me in any direction. During our sessions, I sensed she believed me and believed in me without being judgmental. I left our sessions knowing she supported me and was there for me, even if it wasn't Wednesday at five thirty.

I wrote the following journal entry the day after a terrifying nightmare. Dellene and I had just spoken by phone.

February 23, 2001

I told her Tim made me call. I didn't want to because I had just seen her the night before. She made me laugh . . . "So, you're just going to have your crises on Wednesday at five thirty?" Then she told me she's not here to talk with me for fifty minutes once a week. She's here to walk me through this the whole time. I'm to call her anytime I need to.

She was not judgmental, she believed me and believed in me, she allowed me to be in control, and she was indeed "here to walk me through this the whole time." This was the person I allowed myself to trust.

Open communication with your therapist seems obvious, as you will be sharing your most personal experiences with this person. The difficult piece of open communication for abuse victims is expressing what they need. That requires feeling worthy, something foreign to most victims but imperative to maximizing the benefits of therapy. It took me a long time, and convincing from Dellene, that my needs were important and I was not a burden to her. The following are two of my journal entries documenting those feelings. I wrote the first on a Saturday, a day after I had seen Dellene for a regular session. My memories of abuse kept bubbling up. I was desperate, not wanting to go on, and yet I still didn't want to "bother" her. Tim encouraged me to call, and I met her at the crisis center.

June 1, 2001

I didn't want to go to Dellene. I felt really bad about taking her time again.

That night I had more nightmares, memories of abuse. In the morning I could barely speak, let alone call Dellene. Tim called for me. When she called back, he had to convince me to speak with her. The following entry describes what she said at the end of our conversation, knowing that without Tim, I would not have called.

June 2, 2001

She said we will work on me asking for what I need. I am not a burden on her. She chose this profession. It is not nine to five. She told me, I am your therapist and I am here for you.

Three years later, 2004, marks the first time I have evidence in a journal that I comfortably put my needs first with Dellene. At my preceding therapy session, she had guided me through using visualization techniques to release my intense anger toward Clara and Rune. I had taken two days off from work to recuperate and knew I needed even more time, but I woke up early on a Friday morning riddled with guilt over staying out of work another day. I needed her support.

December 4, 2004

Thursday and Friday I couldn't go to work. I've never been so physically exhausted, aching, barely able to do anything. Of course I jumped to my usual: I should try to go to school Friday. I even called Dellene—woke her Friday at 6:00 AM—because I needed to be told this was that serious, I needed to stay home.

There were many times in the years following when I had to convince myself it was okay to speak up and put my needs first, and

I know there were times when I just couldn't do it. When I did, it always helped my progress toward healing.

Another important time for communicating needs has to do with your surroundings during therapy. Conditions within the therapist's office can trigger anxiety or fear, inhibiting the ability to work on an issue. The scent of a candle, lighting, sounds, or an open window are just a sampling of things that can remind a victim of the conditions surrounding their abuse. They are simple enough to change, if your therapist knows they're troublesome. Therapists are not mind readers. It is up to you to express your needs; it will take time and effort and will create some discomfort. That's okay. Feeling worthy is hard for a victim. Work at it, and express your needs as often as you can. It will get easier once you believe it will make a difference in your progress.

Making a strong, positive connection with your therapist is critical to the therapeutic process. Maintaining control over the direction you are taking, putting your inhibitions aside, and communicating your needs will help foster the trust you need to make that connection.

Connecting with a Spouse or Partner

Whether you are married or in a committed relationship, you will need to connect with your partner on a new level as you make the journey toward healing. If you do not have a significant other, choose a friend or family member who will be your partner throughout your therapy. It is important to have at least one person to confide in and rely on. However, if you are alone or cannot bring yourself to trust another person, healing can still happen for you, though it may be more difficult. Your therapist should know you are working at this alone. If you need additional support, you may choose to join a therapeutic group that deals with issues surrounding sexual abuse. Your therapist can help you find one.

In this section, I'll use my relationship with my husband to illustrate the importance of trust and open communication with a partner. Every relationship is unique, but I hope you will be able to extract ideas from our experience.

If you are sharing your experience with a spouse or partner, a level of trust already exists between the two of you. Whether you've kept your abuse a secret or have repressed your memories of it, the first test of trust will be when you decide to tell your partner. It won't be easy for your partner to learn that the person they love has been sexually abused. If you repressed your memories and they are emerging for the first time, your experience may be even more difficult for your partner to comprehend. As upsetting and confusing as the realization is for you, try to acknowledge how hard it must be for your partner. Agree to work together to understand what has happened to you. You'll need to trust that your partner cares enough about you to believe what you are saying without fully understanding it. That level of trust will become critical to maintaining a relationship throughout your healing journey.

It is also necessary to trust that you can express every emotion with this person. If you are angry, depressed, sad, or emotionally drained, this is not the time to put on a happy face because you are with someone. They need to know what you are feeling so they can help and support you. You need to trust them enough to be yourself.

Your relationship will be challenged throughout your healing journey. Social activities, intimacy, and dependency will change, sometimes within the same day. You can't predict how these changes will affect your relationship. You need to trust that your partner believes you and is committed to helping you. I cannot imagine that I would have made it alone.

I wrote this journal entry following a very painful therapy session. It illustrates Tim's level of commitment and understanding, and my level of trust in him, at a very vulnerable time.

May 30, 2001

Tim walked me through this day. I sat in silence and tears until eleven, determined not to talk to anyone today. He finally encouraged me to try. I felt a little angry, but I did. I told him I wanted to be in silence, that I barely wanted to live. My God, I trust him. He reminded me that this didn't just happen to me last night. It was years ago. That helps some. I asked him to call Dellene for me, say I couldn't talk now but may need her later. He urged me to take a hot shower and said we would go for a ride. I love him so much. It's what makes me want to keep living. I wonder how I can be a mother and teacher, but I don't have to think about being a wife. He just takes care of me. I don't know where I'd be or what would have happened today without him.

Open communication with your partner is also vital throughout your journey to healing. Realize that no matter how much your partner loves you or how smart, well read, or experienced they are, unless they, too, have been sexually abused, they will never understand the extent of your feelings. And that's okay. Try not to get frustrated or angry with them. Do your best to explain your feelings, and then trust they are doing their best to understand.

Following some of my most difficult therapy sessions, Tim would say, "I am so proud of you. You are doing great!" Every time he said it, I cringed inside but never responded. He thought he was being supportive; I thought, *I am not doing great! This is hell—don't you get it?* At the time I was not communicating openly with Tim, but during a therapy session I told Dellene. Later she spoke to Tim and explained why he shouldn't tell me how great I was doing, even though his intentions were wonderful, and that a better response would be to acknowledge that this must be very hard on me.

Another important time to communicate information is following a therapy session. Most partners will want to know at the least how a session went, and at times more detail about what you and your therapist discussed. Share as much as you can, when you can. There were nights when I returned home from a session too exhausted to talk about it. Other times I needed to go straight to my journal and write down the important aspects of the session. Tim often asked how it went when I came in the door but respected a response such as "I just can't talk right now." Following other sessions, I wanted Tim's immediate, undivided attention so that I could share every detail of what Dellene and I had discussed. What is important is that you communicate as much as you are comfortable sharing when you are ready. This approach will equip your partner to help you during the days between sessions.

As with your therapist, communicating your needs to a partner can be difficult because of your diminished sense of self. However, the only way a partner will be able to help you through this healing process is if you express what will help you. Because you are with this person every day, through every phase of healing, countless situations will arise in which it will be important to let your partner know your needs.

The best time to communicate needs is when you *aren't* in crisis. This will take some thought on your part and may be difficult, but it is essential. Some questions to consider in advance:

If you are having nightmares, what do you want your partner to do? Will you wake them? Do you want them to ask you what the nightmare was about? Do you just want to be held in silence?

If you are sad or depressed, do you need to be left alone? Held? Encouraged to let the sadness out?

How about when you are anxious or angry? Should your partner encourage you to release your emotions in a physical way or with medication? Should they stay clear of you?

After each episode of fear, anger, anxiety, or sadness, you may need a different response. That lack of predictability is very hard on a partner. Discuss possible responses so that your partner will have an idea of what to do and can eliminate responses that won't help. I was able to tell Tim that after a nightmare I needed a light on and needed to be held and told repeatedly that I was safe. I told him to ask not, "What was the nightmare about?" but, "Do you want to tell me about the nightmare?"

When I was anxious or exhausted from a session, Tim learned not to suggest that I take a warm bath to relax. Many incidents of my abuse took place in the bathroom and bathtub, so the suggestion only increased my anxiety. Instead, he would ask what I needed. My response usually included getting in bed, drinking a cup of tea, and listening to a Jim Brickman CD.

You may find there's a common denominator in the types of

responses that will help you. For me it was control—the ability to maintain control as long as my decisions kept me safe. I reluctantly agreed to let Tim take control when we agreed it was necessary, but he needed to do so gently, or I'd refuse. With time he learned my preferences for finding comfort. If I was incapable of expressing my needs, he would offer suggestions: *a hot shower might help; why don't you get in bed and I'll put some music on for you; would you like a cup of tea?* By not imposing his ideas on me, he allowed me to maintain control.

There were other times when Tim took control without my input. These were times when I was extremely depressed and not making good choices about eating, medication, or rest. Initially I wasn't okay with it, but I also knew I had no alternative. Shutting down is a great insulator from intense emotional pain, but you can't stay in that state for long. As comforting as it was to sit, stare, and not speak or eat, somehow I knew I had to let Tim step in and take control. Sometimes he would call Dellene and have me speak with her. Other times he would call her and talk to her himself. On one occasion, following one of my most difficult sessions, Tim knew I shouldn't go to work and also knew that if the decision were left to me, I would drag myself in. He picked up the phone and called my principal to say I wouldn't be in the next day.

With time, Tim and I both learned what I needed and what his responses should be. This is all part of the work toward healing. None of it comes naturally, but the benefits of communicating and preparing for situations will help make the process easier.

I wrote the following journal entry one month into therapy. Although Tim and I had been together for years, we found that things that could go unstated between most couples needed to be stated and clarified for us as a couple working through issues of abuse.

February 4, 2001

Dellene's homework for me was to tell Tim about any touch that sets something off in me. No secrets with Tim—very important. Also to tell Tim how much she likes him and what a great job he

is doing for me. He's not controlling—he's listening, he's helping
me take care of myself. She also said to let him know that I need
to be nurtured. Gentle touch, holding, hugging are important.
Tim let me know by taking my hand while I was talking that
he's there—he believes in me—and assured me we will make it
through this.

If you are having issues related to sexual intimacy, there are books
and resources available from experts in the field that you should consider consulting, but I will address the subject briefly here because
we are talking about relationships with a partner or spouse.

Imagine being a young child introduced to sexual acts by an
adult. Your frame of reference becomes fear, confusion, pain,
embarrassment, and disgust. If your abuse happened when you
were a teen or adult who was sexually active prior to the abuse,
your frame of reference changes from excitement, joy, love, and
pleasure to fear, confusion, pain, embarrassment, and disgust.
If your response during the abuse was to dissociate, mentally go
to another place, then your response during sexual intimacy will
probably be the same. You can participate in sex physically without being there mentally. It is also very possible to be unable or
unwilling to have a sexual relationship.

The following entry illustrates my conflicting thoughts in the
aftermath of abuse. I desired sexual intimacy but did not know how
to separate it from the ugly feelings associated with sexual abuse.

April 22, 2002

My mind is so complicated. I love being held, touched, told I'm
loved, but I'm still living inside of a shell. Making love is harder
than ever. I'm intellectualizing about it. How could it be some-
thing beautiful when it was a monstrous fear, pain, shame? How
do I go from victim to wife, lover? How do I erase the tape? I
know what I want with Tim, surrender, but how? It's so hard to
push the ugly feelings away and replace them with good feelings.
Will I ever? Will I be able to work on this? I think so. I want to.

There certainly isn't anyone I trust more than Dellene. I hope I can. Especially for Tim's sake.

Whatever your experience is, it is important to discuss sexual intimacy with your therapist and perhaps to read other books devoted to the topic. I will share a few general suggestions based on my experience and hope you will see the importance of addressing your own needs.

Planning and discussing intimacy with your partner ahead of time can prevent a potentially damaging situation. Being able to speak up in the moment is also critical, because your needs can change in an instant.

During long periods of depression or when your memories of abuse come flooding back, you likely won't be able to have a sexual relationship. This doesn't mean some form of intimacy won't comfort you. Being held, getting a back rub, and sometimes just holding hands feels safe and allows you to feel close to your partner. The key is to communicate that need. An unwanted sexual advance can become a damaging trigger. You can prevent that trigger by letting your partner know how you feel.

Certain touches, kisses, sounds, or scents can also trigger a memory of abuse. As difficult as it is, you must tell your partner when anything causes you to flash back. The first time this happened to me, I was unable to say anything. I just shuddered inside and was left sickened. When I shared the experience with my therapist, she explained that it was critical to my relationship and healing to tell Tim. It was so difficult for me that I had to preface my talk with "Dellene told me I had to tell you . . ." Then Tim knew what *not* to do and also began asking if certain actions were okay. Communicating openly put both of us at ease.

Sexual intimacy may also become difficult for your partner. This is another aspect to discuss with your therapist and with each other. It is not a rejection of you. Your partner is one of many secondary victims of abuse, and their feelings and needs should be addressed.

March 3, 2001

I wanted to be intimate with Tim but he couldn't. In the morning we talked about it. He said he couldn't understand how I could want to. I explained it's a need for intimacy and to know that's not lost from our relationship. I had no idea that it was hard for him because of me. He said, "You are the woman that I love so much and your father molested you. Don't you think that's affecting me?"

Following this conversation, I was upset and unsure of how to respond. I spoke with Dellene about it at my next session.

March 6, 2001

I told her about my week—about Tim. She said to remind him that what happened to me had nothing to do with sex and everything to do with abuse and that it's natural that I still need sexual intimacy with him but for now on my terms—when and how I can.

I did share those thoughts with Tim. It helped us both to keep in mind that the abuse I endured had nothing to do with sexual intimacy.

As open as I am in this book, I feel the complete story of recognizing and repairing the damage sexual abuse did to my sexual relationship with my husband is our private story. I'll tell you that through years of communicating and through working at understanding each other and building trust, we're able to enjoy sexual intimacy without the intrusion of the scars of abuse. It takes work, but you can overcome the obstacles and have a relationship that's complete.

One final thought on your relationship with a partner or spouse: If they have committed to helping you, then their life is going to change, because you will not be the same—not during therapy and perhaps not ever. During difficult times, your social life might come to a halt. The person your partner enjoyed going out with, laughing with, having fun with will be immersed in sadness, anxiety, anger, or depression. Household chores and child-rearing responsibilities that you shared as a couple may be left for your partner to shoulder alone. Just as you need a respite from the work of a survivor, so do they. If your partner needs a night out, weekend away, or a few hours alone, don't get angry—work it out.

There were times when Tim wanted to get away for an evening or weekend but it wasn't wise for me to be alone. We asked a close friend of mine to be his backup. If he needed to go out for an evening, she came to visit or we planned to go out. If he went away for a weekend, she stayed at our house. Having a plan meant that Tim could take the time he needed to rejuvenate without worrying about me.

Open communication between a survivor at work and a partner takes patience, commitment, time, and many mistakes. I'd like to say that if you do A, B, and C it will be easy, but I can't. What I can tell you is that the more you work at expressing your needs, the easier it gets and the more likely you will be to heal and connect with your partner in a whole new way.

I have a loving husband who supported every step of my journey to healing. I'm blessed to have him in my life. Other partners may not have as astute an understanding or as high a level of commitment, but whatever support they can offer will become a blessing to you during the most difficult times on your journey.

Another essential component of your healing journey is open communication between your therapist and your partner. Therapists maintain confidentiality with their clients. This is paramount to a client's ability to share, release, and express whatever is necessary to heal. Giving your therapist and partner permission to communicate with each other is also vital to the healing process and requires you to trust both your therapist and your partner. If you need to maintain control, you can ask that they first discuss with you what they will share with each other. A caveat to this arrangement is an understanding that if you are in danger of hurting yourself, the main concern should be keeping you safe. If that means your therapist and your partner talk without your knowledge, then that's what must happen.

Giving Dellene and Tim my permission to communicate became helpful to all three of us at various times during my therapy. I benefited during the times when I was too upset to talk about something but wanted Tim to know.

May 30, 2001

When I realized I'd be telling Tim, I started to cry. I could barely ask but I asked if she could call him, tell him for me. She said yes and thought he should pick me up. I couldn't drive.

I wrote that the first time I remembered that Rune had raped me. It was at a session with Dellene. I wanted Tim to know, but I could not bear the pain of saying the words again. Dellene took the burden from me by calling Tim, explaining what I had revealed, and asking him to come pick me up. When he arrived, she left Tim and me alone for a while. I was able to cry and be comforted without having to say the words.

Giving permission for Tim to call Dellene was beneficial during those times when he was not sure how to help me. Dellene would explain what might be best for me at that time: let me be in control, exert some control by suggesting things, or take over control. She also advised and supported Tim when he needed to share information with our children. There will be times during therapy when you are not communicating because of fear or depression, or when your behaviors are out of the ordinary or concerning, and your partner will need someone to talk to for reassurance and advice. There is no better person to provide that support than your therapist.

For Dellene, having permission to speak with my partner allowed her to keep a closer eye on me and have more of a hand in helping me.

Connecting with Others

As committed as your therapist and partner may be, there will be times when they can't be there for you. If you are comfortable expanding your support network, I recommend including one other person: a close friend or relative. You must trust that this person will uphold your decision to break your silence and face the difficult task of healing, and that they will keep confidential any information you share. Other personality traits may also be important to you as you select this friend or relative. Take time to think about these kinds of qualities before you make your choice. For example, some of my friends initially questioned why I would want to "dredge up" my past. Because I did not have the energy to defend my decision, I knew they were not the right people to be by my side.

For me, the right person was Nancy. As friends and coworkers, we already had a relationship involving trust. I knew she would keep confidential anything I shared with her. She was a good listener and easy to talk to, as well as a woman of faith and compassion—qualities important to me.

The role that your own friend or relative plays in your healing process will vary based on your needs. The only way they will know how to help you is through your communication with them. If they make suggestions for you, it is important that you express whether you agree or not. I'll share a few specific ways in which Nancy stepped in to supplement the roles of my therapist and partner. Some of her support evolved naturally. She was my confidant at work. Most days we met before school for a quick check-in. If it had been a tough night, I'd share what had happened. She helped me refocus on my job and checked up on me throughout the day. Having someone in the building who knew my fragile state gave me strength to get through it.

On other occasions, I requested Nancy's help. When Tim needed a respite, Nancy took his place. More than once, she slept at our house so I wouldn't be alone if I had a nightmare. Other times she stayed with me for the few hours Tim was out. Her companionship kept me safe and put Tim at ease about getting some space.

Nancy also suggested wonderful ideas for physical activity, which can be a safe means of releasing anger. Most times I was willing to give them a try. She became my partner on the racquetball court, long bike rides, and intense power walks. She encouraged me to sweat, curse, or verbalize my feelings while working out and provided much-needed hugs when these sessions ended.

One of the most comforting supports Nancy provided was prayer. We shared similar religious beliefs, and she was very comfortable praying with me and for me.

June 3, 2001

Nancy and I were supposed to go to a retirement party. I knew it wasn't possible. I wanted badly to be in a church. I also knew it was something Nancy would gladly do with me.

We found a church in a town a ways from where I lived so I did not have to worry about seeing someone I knew.

The Lutheran minister, in the process of locking up the church, agreed to wait and keep it open if we weren't too long. We went in, sat. I thought, *This isn't going to work.* Then I started to cry. Nancy put her arm around me and walked me through prayer. "What do you want to pray for?" *Courage strength peace faith guidance joy relief.* I cried and cried as we prayed. Not only did she selflessly give up her plans to attend the party, she also knew I needed to access my faith for strength—and she made that possible.

References to my spiritual beliefs are woven throughout this book. I am a woman of faith, and my faith played a significant role in my surviving and healing from abuse. While this idea may not resonate with nonbelievers, for those who do believe, I hope it reminds you that there is a greater power to lean on and you are not alone.

When I look back on my life, I see it in segments: my childhood, when the abuse occurred; the thirty-plus years when I repressed my memories of abuse; and my healing journey. My faith was integral to all three.

From the first time I was sexually abused, the sacred was torn from my life. In an instant I lost my childhood and the two people who were meant to love and protect me: my mother and father. I'm often asked how I survived as a little girl. During actual incidents of abuse, I know that my mind went somewhere far away to escape the terror and pain. Psychologists explain this phenomenon as dissociation; I explain it as God protecting me. My vision is of Him taking me away in his arms until the episode was over.

The second question I'm frequently asked is if I'm angry with God for letting this happen to me—a common response to any traumatizing situation. My answer is *no*. We are all born with free will. People make horrific choices every day—hence the evil in the world. My parents chose to abuse me. Clara and Rune hurt me, but they did not destroy the essence of who I am. I believe that God protected my very core, keeping me strong until I was able to face my demons on my own.

During a span of thirty-five years, when I was repressing my memories of abuse, my faith took a few turns. I questioned my beliefs, as most young people do; I stayed away from organized religion for several years; and finally I chose to become an active member of the Methodist Church. Although I lived with unexplained self-doubt, that was a time span in which I built a strong career and relationships, as well as a family of my own—all of which helped to create the foundation I needed to unveil those memories and begin my healing journey. I believe God had a plan, and that plan was to surround me with the people I would need for the next segment of my life.

It's no coincidence that after I went through one failed marriage, Tim came into my life. It's evident throughout this book that he is an amazingly selfless man who had the insight to support every step of my journey. It still amazes me today that when I first told him that Rune sexually abused me, after Tim had already lived with me for more than twenty years, he never, *ever* doubted my words. If he had, I would have used his doubt to run from the truth. I believe that God put Tim in my life and gave him the tools to give me unending support.

It is also no coincidence that Dellene became my therapist. I believe she was placed in my path because she was the perfect person for me—experienced with issues of sexual abuse, compassionate, committed, and one who gently guides, not controls, the course of therapy.

I believe in a higher power; for me, that higher power is God. I have relied on prayer my entire life and have faith that in time my prayers will be answered. My faith has given me strength when I felt emptied of strength, and hope when I felt hopeless. One of my most profound realizations came when I was nearly destroyed by the thought that I had no mother or father in the true sense of the words. In a moment of despair, this thought came to me: *I am God's daughter, and yes, He is my mother and my father, and that brings me peace.*

I hope you will find comfort in your own faith and in knowing that you are never alone.

My faith and my three lifelines—Dellene, Tim, and Nancy—combined forces in my healing journey to achieve a common outcome: they encouraged me and gave me courage, they fought for me to go on when I was close to giving up, and by believing in me, they showed me that I could believe in myself. I know that the burden on my husband, my therapist, and my friend during this tumultuous time was sometimes greater than I can imagine. But depending on and stepping in to relieve one another helped renew their strength and mine. I am so thankful that all of them accepted that responsibility. The following journal entry summarizes my gratitude.

June 4, 2001

Dear Lord, thank you for your presence in my life today. Thank you for Nancy, with whom I can openly speak and share my faith; for Tim, who is my life, my savior; for Dellene, without whom I would never make it.

Eventually it will become necessary to share information with additional family members and friends as they begin to suspect something is wrong. If you are experiencing changes in your social habits, affect, or physical looks, they are going to notice the change. If they're true friends or loving family members, they will want to support you but may be reluctant to ask how to.

Choose carefully with whom you will share, and do it when you feel ready. Talk about it with your therapist and partner ahead of time. Understand that you are doing this for yourself. You can't predict how others will react, but you can control whom you tell and how much information you share.

June 24, 2001

Dellene said it would be helpful if I broaden my base of people who know. I could tell Joyce—we've known each other for thirty years, I trust her, and yet I'm debating. Dellene thinks I shouldn't "plan" it. If I'm with someone and it feels right, I tell. If not, I don't.

Joyce and I were meeting the next morning for breakfast. I predicted I wouldn't tell her. But, as Dellene surmised, the time was right.

June 25, 2001

Well, my guess was wrong. I told Joyce. At breakfast I was not myself at all. I suggested we go to a park. Then I told her. She cried and listened. It was good for me. Good to talk and she was very supportive.

A part of my need to tell came from my strong desire to stop pretending. I had pretended my whole life that I had the perfect childhood. I just couldn't keep up the facade any longer. When I struggled to make conversation with my friend at breakfast, I knew it was time to share.

Sometimes a situation will arise that makes it necessary to tell your story right then, rather than waiting until the time is "right." Six weeks after I started therapy, a group of my girlfriends who'd been getting together for years were planning an overnight at one friend's house. No one knew what I was dealing with. I wanted to go but feared being without someone to support me during the night. Tim, Dellene, and I all agreed it would be good for me to have this diversion, but only if I talked with one of the girls prior to that night. I made the decision to tell, chose the person, and made a plan to meet.

February 19, 2001

The visit with Jake was so good. She arrived with yellow tulips and a big hug. I was nervous and stumbling and finally said one thing about Rune. She grabbed my hands in hers and said, I knew this was what you were going to tell me. I cried a lot, we cried a lot. It felt so good to have her hold me, not think I was crazy, accept me and be there to help. I have to be the luckiest woman. Tim, Nancy, Jake—I feel so loved and supported and that's what will get me through.

Each time I told someone, the time prior to our meeting made me anxious, and in the hours afterward I was emotionally drained, but I also realized that the support and love of friends renewed my strength. Having close friends be aware of my situation made it easier both to decline social invitations and to be with them, because I no longer had to pretend everything was okay.

Being open will also provide your friends with a sense of relief. As much as they won't want to hear you were sexually abused, it is better than knowing something is wrong but not knowing what. In June 2001, five months into my therapy with Dellene, our son graduated high school. Nancy was the only guest at the graduation party who knew what I was facing. Months later, when Tim and I told one couple who were dear friends, the wife shared her recollection: "After the graduation party, I cried all the way home. You looked so thin and drawn. I told John I knew something was terribly wrong with you."

Most people won't know how to react after your initial talk, but their silence doesn't mean they do not support you. They just don't know what to do. If phone calls or spending time together will help, you need to communicate that need. If you can't handle questions, you need to say so.

Many of my friends stopped calling or asking if I wanted to get together. Instead they started sending cards and notes of encouragement—just the comfort I needed. I didn't have to talk with them or share more than I wanted in order to feel their support. I saved every card as a reminder of how blessed I was to have caring friends in my time of need. One of my favorites was a note from my cousin. I came home from an exhausting day, feeling sad, to find that an envelope had arrived in the mail, with this handwritten note inside:

> Hi Bob,
> Thinking of you!
> Consider this note a hug. Not the "nice to see you" kind of hug, but the –
> "I love you" kind of hug!
> Chrissy –

Imagine being sad, depressed, and worn and then opening this letter. It made all the difference in my day then and still warms my heart now.

There will be times when you will need more from your friends. You'll feel desperate to have someone understand the hell you are living through or to help you escape from that hell. You may be conflicted, too exhausted to go anywhere, but wishing someone would call to invite you out. You won't want to talk but will long for a friend to call to see how you are. Healing takes years and elicits a roller coaster of emotions. The best way to maintain relationships with friends and benefit from their support is to explain the inconsistency of your needs based on your emotional state. Let them know that it is okay to call as long as they understand that sometimes you'll want to talk and other times you won't be up to it. If this desire is too difficult for you to express, as it was for me, you can ask your partner to do the explaining for you. At one point during the second year of my healing journey, Tim sent an e-mail to some of my closest friends, explaining that this was what I needed. It helped both my friends and me.

As time goes on, connecting in a new way with friends will become easier. When you are stronger, you will be able to express your needs, and your friendships will settle into a comfortable place in your life. Those who really care about you will stay with you through the rough spots and do their best to understand. I instantly had the support of some friends, while others took time. Some never understood. It is those last few who make it necessary to share this next, difficult section.

Disconnecting

As important as it is to maintain relationships on this journey, it is equally important to let go of relationships that do not contribute to your well-being. One way to assess the value of a friendship is to ask yourself, *Is this person's presence in my life aiding my healing process or blocking my healing?* If the person is hindering your ability to heal, you need to think about disconnecting. As you work through therapy, some friendships will fade on their own, just as they do when people move to a new state, get divorced, or change jobs. It is a natural process that shouldn't cause you harm or pain.

The close friends who are not able to support you during this time in your life may withdraw themselves for a variety of reasons. Perhaps they have had a similar experience but are unwilling or unable to talk about it or to do the work you are doing to heal. It is possible they don't believe you or don't believe you should have exposed this tragic secret. Whatever the case, something is blocking them from being able to support you, listen to you, or be true friends to you during this tumultuous time, and it is better to end these relationships than to continue in the hope that these people will understand and react differently.

I experienced firsthand both the difficulty and the relief involved in disconnecting from close friends. My husband and I were very close to a particular couple. We socialized for many years, spent time together on holidays, and knew each other's families. When I first started dealing with my abuse, Tim and I chose not to tell our friends. A few months into my therapy, we stopped socializing almost entirely, which meant we saw this couple only on occasion. Other friends inquired whether everything was okay, and little by little we told people what we were dealing with.

Several months passed without our hearing from this couple. It bothered me enough that I gathered my courage and called the wife to tell her about my abuse and therapy. Her response was awkward but conveyed concern. She uttered, "Oh, oh my" a few times but never asked any questions. The conversation was one-sided and brief. Following that phone call, I never heard from her.

My first reaction was to be upset that she never called to see how I was. My second reaction—so typical of a victim—was guilt: *I* should be calling *her* and letting her know how I was. Out of guilt, I'd make that call, and we'd have a strained conversation that ended with her saying, "Call us if you feel up to getting together." This cycle—no phone call from her, guilt from me, and then my call—went on for a year and left me with a nagging feeling: *Why aren't they calling?* Finally, in a Christmas card, more than three years after that first conversation, I wrote, *I'm doing a little better. We miss you and would love to see you, but I need for you to call to make a plan.*

I was ready to socialize but not up to taking the initiative. The phone never rang. After talking it over with Tim, I realized this relationship didn't support my healing process; it caused only guilt and disappointment. The healthiest resolution for me was to let it go.

You may find yourself in a similar predicament with one or more of your friends. Part of the healing process is to learn to take care of yourself and respect your feelings. Making the decision to disconnect from a relationship that detracts from that process means you are moving forward in a healthy direction.

Ending the Relationship

The next step, ending an unhealthy relationship, is the most difficult. Ideally, I would advise making a plan with your partner or therapist to do so. Rehearse your conversation and then make the call. Stress that the most important focus in your life right now is to heal, and that you need to be surrounded by people who can support that process. Let the friend know how their response to you—or lack thereof—makes you feel, and that, at least for now, it would be best to end the relationship. This approach puts you in control and is an honest, admirable way to disconnect.

Note that I did say *ideally* that is my advice. However, I wasn't able to follow my own advice when I ended my relationship with this couple. Once I realized the need to move on, I stopped calling. Since they weren't contacting me anyway, the relationship ended. At the time, I did not have the courage or energy to be direct, so I believe it was the best decision. I missed the friendship we'd had in the past, but not the strained conversations and guilt.

A final thought on disconnecting with friends: it isn't a matter of judgment or thinking they are "bad people." It is a matter of making healthy choices that will aid in your healing journey and considering what works for you without adding stress to your life. I don't harbor bad feelings toward the couple I disconnected from. I can surmise why they were uncomfortable with my decision to break my silence, but I will never know for sure. What I do know is that they were truly my friends at one point and they did not intend to hurt me in any way. That is an important thought to hold on to if you are faced with disconnecting from a friend.

Other relationships can be much more damaging and will have to end in order for you to heal. I call these people perpetuators of dysfunction. Who falls into this category? Your abuser, and people who know and still support your abuser.

You may be surprised that I include the abuser in this group.

Sadly, some survivors remain in the company of the person who abused them. If a child was abused by a relative, the child may see that person at family gatherings for years after the abuse stops. A college student may still see their abuser in classes or on campus. If someone was molested by a coworker and kept silent, they might still see that person at work. Regardless of the situation, if an abuser remains present in a survivor's life, it is unlikely that the survivor will ever feel completely healed and whole. Some survivors believe they have forgiven their abuser and can lead healthy lives in their presence. I cannot speak to that, but I can discuss the need to disconnect from the perpetuators of dysfunction and the process of doing so.

The Need to Disconnect

I did something to deserve this. I am not worthy of being treated any other way. I was at fault. They didn't know any better; they didn't mean to hurt me. I feel guilty, ashamed, frightened, damaged. Everything's okay. Pretend. Lie. Block it out. No one will believe me; no one cares.

This is an example of a tape that plays over and over in the mind of a survivor. Can that tape be erased if the survivor is in the presence of their abuser or someone who supports the abuser? My response is *no!* These thoughts were on automatic rewind in my mind for most of my life and are shared by nearly every person—male, female, adult, or child—who has experienced sexual abuse. The saddest part is, none of those statements is true. They are merely evidence of the damage and dysfunction engraved in our minds as a result of abuse.

It takes years of work to erase such negative statements, but the end result is a smooth stone on which positive affirmations can be written. What a beautiful thought: the dysfunctional tape can be replaced by statements like *I did not deserve this. I am a survivor, healed and whole. My abuser did not ruin me or take my life from me. I am loved and capable of loving. There is joy in my life!*

I live with my "stone" cleansed and engraved with positive affirmations because I did the work and disconnected from my perpetuators of dysfunction. This was the hardest phase of my therapy—harder than reliving my memories of abuse, harder than visualizing my deceased abuser, harder than any anger or pain I experienced. As painful as it was, I know now that if I had not ended my relationship with some members of my biological family, I would not be living my life as a thriving survivor now.

I'll use the example of Clara, my mother, to illustrate the rationale, process, and outcome of disconnecting. It can be as difficult to disconnect with someone who has hurt you as it is to end a relationship with someone who has loved you. Abusive people are manipulative, and if you've lived under their spell, fear and guilt may cause you to doubt your decision. Disconnecting is also a process that takes time. The greatest hind causing me to stay connected to Clara was my longing for her to transform from a vile abuser into a loving parent. My wish never came true. Ultimately, my courage to disconnect from Clara was fueled by my desire to live. But as strong as that desire was, my disconnection from my mother had to happen in stages.

Stage One: Telling Clara

Eight months into my therapy, Tim, Dellene, and I agreed it was time for me to tell Clara about my memory of being sexually abused by Rune. Up to that point, she had had no idea of what I was going through. I could no longer pretend everything was fine when in fact I was anxious, not sleeping, reliving memories of abuse, and beginning to realize that Clara had known about it, had been in the house when it went on, and had done nothing to stop him. I prepared for the meeting in a session with my therapist.

August 10, 2001

We talked a lot about talking to my mother. This is not a debate. I do not have to defend myself. I have to state the facts—she knew. She did nothing to protect me. I can hear what she has to say and that's it. Regardless of her denial, these are the facts. Dellene said it will be the process of telling my mother that will be good for me. I will be strong and feel stronger after.

Dellene stressed the importance of doing this for myself, not for Clara's reaction.

The next day, August 11, 2001, I went to the house where I grew up and confronted the woman whose role was to protect me. I told her what I remembered and questioned why she did nothing to stop Rune from abusing me. A few of her responses, taken from my journal, say it all: "I'm shocked. I didn't know. Don't you think I would have done something if I knew? So much went on here—his drinking, Grandpa living with us—how could I have known?" And the most disturbing comment she made: "How many times did he cheat on me?" Not only did she deny knowing, she equated her husband's sexually abusing her child with "cheating." In the hour we talked, she never once reached out to comfort me.

This first stage of telling Clara offered me some relief because I no longer had to pretend everything was fine. Her responses abetted my fears that she had known about the abuse all along.

Stage Two: Setting Boundaries

During the days and months following that conversation, I wavered between anger and guilt. Clara told me I was ruining her life, ruining our family. Every time I spoke with her or saw her, I had a twinge of hope that this would be the day she'd say, "I'm so sorry I let this happen to you." That was all I needed to hold on to a relationship with her. But, as Dellene told me over and over, hope dies hard. Clara's apology never came. Instead, she continued to tell me how much my revelations upset her life and never asked how I was doing. In her words, "If I admitted I knew, that would make me a bad mother, and I wasn't a bad mother."

Clara's refusal to accept responsibility was yet another denial for me. She denied me the protection I deserved as her child, and she denied me now as an adult. As painful as this realization was, I was still not ready to end my relationship with her, so the next logical step was to set boundaries. After discussing it in a session with Dellene, I decided to tell Clara not to call me. If I wanted to speak with her, I would call her. When I did call, I did not want to hear how hard this was for her.

Setting boundaries acted as a one-way Band-Aid. Clara's comments couldn't get in to hurt me, but that didn't stop my own pain from building inside. Something was fighting its way to the surface. The more I remembered about Clara and my childhood, the more destructive maintaining a relationship with her became—yet I was still afraid to let go of her.

Stage Three: Facing the Truth

I *knew* the truth: Clara was not going to admit to knowing Rune abused me. I just didn't want to face that truth. If I said it out loud, I would have to do something about it; if I continued to hide from the truth, it would eventually destroy me. The following journal entry describes my desperate state.

June 22, 2001

My mother is doing a job on my mental state. I won't say much to Tim or Dellene because Tim is so angry with her already and Dellene will make me work on it. That's a very scary thought to me. It would lead to breaking all family ties. I'd feel terrible for my kids. How will I ever deal with this?

Tim's feelings toward Clara, Dellene's "making" me deal with it, and the ways in which disconnecting would affect my children were all excuses to escape the reality: I needed to disconnect from Clara or I would never be healed and whole.

It took almost another year of occasionally seeing Clara, talking about her in therapy, struggling with anger and depression, and, most important, holding on to the hope that she'd one day acknowledge the abuse and apologize, before the most disturbing memories emerged for me.

May 1, 2002

A new chapter. Clara. What stories will be told? Looking at the name, I see: cold, hard, cruel, rejecting. I feel a tightness in my throat, a physical restriction, holding down emotion, push down the pain and anger, force it in. My heart pounds just thinking of it.

Did you know she was actually a part of this? She didn't just hide her eyes, she participated. Took an active role. No one knows this yet. It is yet to be revealed. I let on to Dellene and then Tim by just saying I fear I may find this out. I can only say all this in my own quiet protected world, not out loud. This part is going to take incredible strength.

This was the beginning of the next step toward disconnecting with Clara. Dreams, visions, and memories were all telling me she had participated in the abuse. The thoughts were destroying me, and yet I couldn't express them. When I couldn't contain the emotional pain any longer, I sought relief from physical pain by digging my fingernails into the palms of my hands. I had to tell Dellene about my memories of Clara's involvement, for fear that I would otherwise turn to more damaging forms of self-injury.

May 8, 2002

By the time I got to Dellene's I was choking, anxious, a mess. It took a few minutes. I told her about Clara's role in the abuse. The hurt was unbearable. How strong am I supposed to be? I can't take it. I have nothing to hold on to. Over and over I asked, What did she get out of it? Why?

Stage Four: Speaking Up

Setting boundaries and facing the truth of Clara's involvement in the abuse weren't enough. I couldn't stop thinking about my abusive mother and the emotions that experience raised. As a little girl, I was unable to speak up, unable to express my fear and pain, unable to protect myself. It was time to speak up for that little girl and tell Clara how I felt.

With Dellene's help, we planned a meeting at her office with Clara and Clara's therapist. The purpose was for me to say everything I needed to say to Clara without sugarcoating it or, as I had done my whole life, trying to be the good daughter. The preparation for this meeting took several sessions. I needed to release the anger before I would be able to say the words. I wrote what I wanted to say and practiced saying the words out loud. Nancy and I role-played the actual meeting. Though I was frightened and at times doubted what I planned to do, I still knew this was a necessary step for healing. Each time she denied me, I became victimized again. If I wanted the abuse to stop, I had to stop it myself. The following journal entry expresses my fear as I prepared for the meeting.

August 19, 2002

Why can't I let it out? Let it rip? Why can't I hate her? Am I going to let someone stab me over and over for the rest of my life? Wake up. She's not going to protect you, save you, be there for you. Face it! I feel like such an ass. Just do it—let her go. God help me!

Dellene's words resonated: *Hope dies hard.*

August 22, 2002, finally arrived. My hands were sweating, my mouth dry, my heart pounding, and yet I had the courage of a lioness defending her cub as I faced this woman, my mother. I recounted multiple incidents of abuse: my recollection of his first attempt, at the cottage, when he climbed into the bunk and groped me; the countless nights he appeared at the foot of my bed to molest me; Rune's invading my privacy in the bathroom to satisfy his sick desires. Letting her know I knew she was there, allowing the abuse to continue. This journal entry is a sketch of that empowering encounter.

August 22, 2002

Then I started—the cottage and that the abuse could have ended there. The bedroom, bathroom, verbal comments, her being there, in the bedroom, silent, holding the door shut . . .

She responded with denials and accusations.

No, no, I don't remember. No, I didn't do that. Why can't I remember?

And then the question that nearly pushed me over the edge.

How after forty-one years can you remember all of this and with such detail?

I leaned forward and responded. Because it's the terror and horror that happened to me. Sometimes I remember detail, sometimes only the feeling of his naked body against mine. Sometimes I don't let myself remember the details because I can't f'in take it—it's too painful.

She cowered and put her hands over her eyes—no tears.

I told her I couldn't take the abuse any longer. I had to make a choice. I had wanted to leave my family, end my life; now I chose life, my family. Those were my final words.

When Dellene and I were alone, we processed the encounter.

I did it! I said all I wanted and planned to say. Clara's response confirmed that I had to let go and move on. She left no reason for hope.

The relief following that meeting lasted a short time. It was like unlocking the door to a room filled with trash. Once some of the trash dribbled out, the rest came tumbling out behind it. I had more nightmares and more memories of Clara's abusive behavior. The greatest outpouring was one of anger and pain, over the realization that I did not have a mother and never had. A mother loves, nurtures, and protects her young. Clara did none of those things.

For the next fifteen months, I released emotions in healthy ways, such as physical activity, talking with my three lifelines, and journaling, and sometimes unhealthy ways, such as speeding down the highway, walking alone through the woods, blasting music to drown out my screams—all of which I did alone, without the safety net of a partner. I denied the truth of Clara's role in my abuse, and I faced the reality with great courage. I worked through every high and low with Dellene and Tim by my side. The realization that Clara was as sick as

Rune had been was destroying me. I had to find a way to cope. They had destroyed my childhood; I could not allow them to destroy my life as an adult.

Stage Five: Cutting the Cord

Maintaining a relationship with Clara kept the abuse alive. Every time I spoke with her, I slipped back into the dysfunction of guilt, my own denial that Clara was that bad, and the belief that I deserved what they'd done to me. But I had the power to stop the abuse, and it was time to exert that power.

Based on my need for control and closure, Dellene, Tim, and I developed a plan. I'd go back to the house where the abuse took place, where Clara still lived. I needed to walk through every room, face the demons of my past, and put to rest my childhood of abuse. I needed to bring peace to that little girl who lived in silent terror. We chose a weekend when Dellene was working at the crisis center. I'd be able to speak with her before I went to the house and could see her afterward. Tim would drive me and wait in the car. Once our safe plan was in place, we made arrangements with Clara. I called and said I needed to come to the house Sunday to see her. She never questioned why, which was a relief for me. I wanted to save everything I needed to say for that day.

On November 2, 2003, I disconnected with the woman who was my mother and the perpetuator of abuse and dysfunction.

Before I arrived at the house, my anxiety, fear, and anger felt unbearable. I stayed completely still, staring straight ahead as Tim drove. I remember having to tell myself to breathe. Tim reached for my hand, sending a silent message that I was not alone.

But once inside, I was in a state of control, courageously forthcoming. I walked through each room where Rune molested me and restated what each parent had done. I told Clara about every painful event that had gone on for years.

November 2, 2003

I am free. I did it. I faced my demons! I am physically and emotionally drained. My body is weak and aches but I need to write. Tim and I went to church. I needed strength. I spoke with Dellene for support and encouragement and then we left. I said then and now, no one deserves to feel what I felt on that ride. The anxiety, anger, and fear over needing to do this were unbearable. We arrived. Tim waited in the car and I went in.

I told Clara I have to see this house. "Go ahead, walk around." I went to my old bedroom. Come here, look, that's where he knelt when he used to touch my breasts. That's where he tried to force himself on me. That's where he raped me, and you, you stood right here and closed the door. "No! How could you dream up all these things?" Dream them up! I lived them. No one could dream up what I lived through. I walked to the bathroom. Come here. Look! Look at that tub. He used to get in it while I was on the toilet. "And where was I?" Right out here, in the living room. "No! No!" Look in here. He used to fondle me in that tub. Look at this toilet. He would kneel on the floor next to me and rub his hands up my thighs. We moved into the living room. Look at that chair. He sat there and you stood right there as he was kissing me and forcing my hand on his crotch and you yelled Rune what are you doing? I ran to my room. Where were you? Why didn't you come and comfort me, tell me he was wrong, get rid of him! "Because I didn't know. I didn't know. Why can't I remember these incidents? I've tried." Because you don't want to remember. All you ever cared about was the shell of this house. Pretending nothing was wrong, the perfect housewife, perfect Girl Scout leader, not letting on to a husband who was an alcoholic and a child molester. You closed your eyes to it then and you are closing your eyes to it now.

I got up to look at the bedroom again and started to cry. The bed, my doll, still there, the spindles on the headboard that I used to grip made my heart pound. I heard her come toward me. "Can I put my arms around you?" No! Don't touch me! I went toward the bathroom and cried even more. "I just want to put my arms around you." It's too late! Why didn't you put your arms around me then, when I needed you? "Because I didn't know." The first memory I have of him coming after me we were staying at the cottage. It was dark, he came in and was all over me. You came in and pulled him off of me. I was three or four years old. That was the last and only time you did anything to protect me. You never came back in the room to hold me, comfort me. I was your child! You denied me then and you deny me now!

When we returned to the kitchen, where we'd started, Clara began asking about my husband and children as if the past thirty minutes hadn't occurred. Once again, she pretended everything was fine; once again, she denied my feelings.

Finally, there came a moment when something seemed to dawn on her.

"Wait, so does this mean you never want to see me again? Is this it? You don't want any communication from me? You'll never see me again?"

I stood in silence, gathering the courage to respond while realizing the end had come. My response: "That's up to me to decide." And I walked out the door, never to return to that house or see Clara again.

Disconnecting brought about a new beginning for me. Although I still went through a few dark times dealing with the loss of a father, a mother, and a childhood, I felt free. I had my feelings of grief to deal with, but never again would these sick parents hurt me. I took control and ended the abuse that had nearly destroyed my life. The experience empowered me, allowing me to put the little girl to rest— protected, safe, and never to be abused again. My healing would not have been complete without this final event.

Summary

If a perpetuator of dysfunction is keeping you entrenched in the past, keeping you tied to your abuse, even if by a thread, you need to consider disconnecting. The process of doing so can take on many forms: in person, in a letter, through visualization with a therapist, or in whatever other way is appropriate for the situation and for you. Whether it happens in stages or all at once, you must carefully plan the process of disconnecting, as it may be the most difficult step in your healing journey.

I was almost ready to give up on my life when I found the strength to take the most important step on my own journey. I opted to expose this very painful stage in the hope that I can empower others to disconnect from the perpetuators of dysfunction in their own lives and to experience the joy of healing for themselves.

Part II:
Tools for the Journey

"Tools for the Journey" is devoted to the three fundamental strategies I used on my healing journey. They've become a part of my repertoire for handling life's challenges beyond healing.

4
Creating a Respite

The word *respite* is defined as *a usually short interval of rest or relief.* In the context of this book, a respite is a brief time when your mind is not embedded in thoughts of abuse, treatment, and emotional pain and life resembles normalcy.

The journey to healing is long and can consume your whole being. You can be wrapped up in the various stages of therapy twenty-four hours a day, seven days a week. And yet if you remain in this intense state of awareness, you will soon be devoid of any emotional and physical energy to go on. But the reality is that life will go on regardless. Jackson Browne's song title "Running on Empty" puts words to this thought. You cannot put the demands of your family and your job on hold just because you are running on empty. Your children still need to be cared for, and your bills need to be paid. So how do you manage your life and find the time or place to refuel? How do you put the most invasive time of your life aside long enough to give you the respite you need to regain strength?

The first step is to realize you'll have to *create* this respite. You will not wake up some mornings and feel free from your healing journey. A great wave will not come along, lifting you on the tide. Nor will you look back on a given day and say, "Wow, I never thought about my situation all day." It just doesn't work that way. Once you decide to face your demons and work toward healing, you will be immersed, so you must create a place where your mind and body will take a rest from the all-consuming life of a survivor at work.

There may be a place that already serves as a respite without your realizing it: your place of employment, a weekly church service, or someone's home you like to visit. The possibilities are there; you just need to become aware that they are your respite.

My work was this place for me. Never in my thirty-three years of teaching did I think I would call my job a respite, but that is exactly what it became once I committed to therapy, though I didn't recognize it as such for a long time. I used to think life would be easier if I didn't have such a great responsibility to face every day, but after months in therapy, I came to the realization that going to work each day was helping me, not hurting me. Five days a week, from seven thirty to four thirty, I could count on being distracted from my personal life. The distraction wouldn't last the full nine hours, but for a large part of that time, my mind and energy would be focused on my job: teaching. Children demand attention, and that was just what I needed: someone or something forcing my thoughts surrounding abuse and therapy into the background. Even though I expended energy at work, it was not the same draining energy involved in thinking of, talking about, experiencing the pain of abuse.

Whether you're working in a store, an office, a hospital, or a factory, or you're volunteering, you have certain responsibilities. Someone is depending on you to do your job. It is important to allow yourself to recognize your value in the workplace. This perception may require a conscious effort. Victims of abuse are not the first people to stand up and say, "We're valuable!" Yet recognizing your value and giving precedence to your job responsibilities will give you a rationale for putting your personal strife aside—not for great lengths of time, just long enough to give your mind and body a rest.

For those who are stay-at-home moms, homemakers, or unemployed, this might be more of a challenge, because you're not physically moving each day to a different setting. Changing your venue can help change your thoughts, so, if possible, find a time each week when you can get away. Volunteering at a school or church, in a hospital, library, or senior center, or working a part-time job are all good options. If this isn't possible, you may have to create your own respite at home. You will learn how to do so later in this chapter, in the section "Creating a Respite."

There are three important strategies to consider when using your place of employment as a respite: the who, the what, and the when of sharing information. All three are in some way related to maintaining control—a respite engineered by you, the conductor.

Sharing Information

The first step is to plan in advance whom you would and would not want to share information with. The decision to take someone into your confidence is highly subjective. When I first began therapy, I had a strictly professional relationship with my school principal. I didn't feel comfortable sharing any level of my personal situation with her. I kept my barriers up, and, fortunately, she did not ask questions. Two years later, a new principal took over. We developed mutual respect and eventually a friendship. I wrote the following journal entry at a time when my anxiety was mounting. I saw Dellene at the crisis center on Saturday and said I felt as though I were living in a vacuum, trying to suck in another memory fighting its way to the surface. We agreed that I would try to access the memory at our session on Monday evening.

September 21, 2004

Driving to work is when I began to feel sick inside. I made a decision to talk to MaryBeth. She needed to know something. My relationship with her is so different than with Cecilia. I think I was predicting that I'd need to be home today. She was great, as I expected.

That Monday, I asked MaryBeth to meet with me after school about a personal matter. I prefaced the conversation by saying that what I had to tell her was difficult to discuss and confidential: "I'm in therapy to address my past of sexual abuse." I shared a few details about my childhood and about my involvement in therapy.

Still struggling with poor self-esteem—so typical of a victim—I was certain my disclosure would result in her losing confidence in me. I stressed that I was capable of leaving my issues at home and not allowing them to affect my performance at work.

MaryBeth's first response was that she felt honored that I shared such a personal struggle with her. She asked what she could do to help and assured me that she would support anything I needed. As a result of our conversation, I was able to be open with her when I needed a day off. And if I had a tough night but still went to work the next day, her understanding look helped put me at ease.

Another important consideration when planning to share information is to choose someone whom you trust to respect your need for privacy. Even some of the nicest people have difficulty keeping a confidence, so choose wisely and clearly state your expectations. My preference was to tell the person that I did not want any confusion or misunderstandings. I welcomed their questions and did my best to provide answers. Preplanning will help you avoid those vulnerable times when you want to stand on a mountaintop and declare to the world that you are suffering. There were days when I wanted to go in to work and tell anyone who would listen, "I'm in emotional pain, I am a victim." But if I had given in to the desire, I'd have regretted it; I wasn't ready to be so exposed. Also, if everyone knew my story and expressed concern, my place of work could no longer be my place of respite.

How much information are you willing to share? The level of disclosure will depend on how well you know and trust the person. It can be as simple as telling someone you are going through a very difficult time in your life. You can set boundaries by requesting that they respect your need for privacy and not ask any further questions. There may be days when you simply need to tell someone you had a tough night. There's comfort in having the right person know you're not at your best. If you can—though only if you feel a strong sense of trust—I suggest you try to share your story in a little more depth. Without revealing details, you can state that you are dealing with issues of sexual abuse.

This became an important step for me in my work environment.

As a special-education teacher and assistant to the principal, I worked with children who were victims of sexual abuse. It was difficult to detach myself emotionally from their situation. I saw myself in each young child and had an unrealistic expectation of being able to save them. If only someone had saved me. Although I refrained from acting on it, my vulnerability compromised my role as an educator. The colleague I chose to share with became sensitive to my needs and avoided involving me in cases related to sexual abuse. Choosing to converse with one person on a more intimate level resulted in a sense of protection within my work environment.

If your job does not have a connection with abuse victims, you still have good reason to share your information with a colleague. A perfect example involves any conversation initiated in the lunchroom or by the water cooler about news items related to sexual predators. High-profile cases of sexual abuse are apt to spark conversation that may be upsetting for you to hear, and a colleague's insensitive comment or joke may trigger your anxiety or anger. Your confidant can be the one to change the conversation or engage you in a private conversation just in time to spare you unneeded stress. Though it is impossible to be prepared for every situation that arises, anticipating some of these scenarios, along with your response to them, will help you to create a respite at work.

When sharing information, you should also consider how you will answer questions from coworkers. I recommend anticipating their questions and planning your answers. I often talked this through with Dellene so I wouldn't be caught off guard. As my therapy went on, I lost weight and lost countless hours of sleep. Most days I didn't look my best, and after a night of crying I looked my worst. It was natural for people to begin asking if I was okay. For a long time, I answered, "Oh, I'm fine. I just didn't sleep well last night," but after a while, those words echoed pretending—the pretending I had done for most of my life that everything was fine.

When I could no longer live with that answer, I changed my response: "No, I'm not okay now, but I will be. Thank you for asking." That statement helped me to be honest without divulging too much. Most people sensed my need for boundaries and did not ask further questions. Maintaining boundaries can be construed as negative or standoffish, but for victims, boundaries are a means of protection and a way to maintain control. I did not want to be perceived as standoffish, but during my difficult years in therapy, it was necessary.

Be aware of the days when it is important to stay away from difficult situations. I learned the hard way. I remember a day when I was raging with anger incited by memories of my abusers. I arrived at work not anticipating that my anger was about to erupt. Early in the day, I met with a colleague to discuss a sensitive but typical school issue. Before I knew what was happening, I heard myself shouting at this teacher, and then I stormed out of his room. A typical conflict at work became the catalyst to ignite my repressed anger. I felt foolish and embarrassed.

I was able to go back a day later and apologize, saying I had been having a bad day. In that instance, with that particular person, apologizing put the situation behind us without damaging our relationship. I learned I needed to be aware of my emotional state before I walked in to work. When I was able to identify anger building, I isolated myself from my colleagues as much as my job would allow. Having an awareness of your emotions can prevent embarrassing situations. The less you have to explain your behavior at work, the better. Remember, you're trying to make work a respite, not a place of added stress.

There will be times when staying away will mean more than just isolating yourself within your workplace; it will mean not going to work at all. It is important to be aware of the need to stay home and surrender to that need when it arises. There will be days when you will feel stripped of all energy—after a difficult session in therapy or a new realization—or overcome with sadness, anger, or exhaustion. On those days, your body will scream at you to take care of yourself—though, again, as a victim of abuse, you may not make self-care your first priority.

Most times I fought my own need to stay home. When I did, it would require much encouragement from Tim, and even then I wouldn't be happy, because I would feel as if I had given in. I thought I was losing control, when in truth, staying home and resting was the only way to rebuild my strength and move forward. If I had gone to work, I wouldn't have been able to function effectively and would have caused myself even greater stress.

It is essential that you learn to listen to your body. If you feel physically or emotionally exhausted, if your body aches from tension or you can't stop crying, it may mean you need a day of rest. Ask yourself if going to work will provide a distraction or if it seems like an insurmountable task. If the answer is the latter, honor your feelings and stay home. It is also essential to relinquish control and listen to someone who cares about you and recognizes your need for intervention. This was never easy for me, and often led to my being angry at the one person who knew what I needed most, but once I accepted Tim's advice to stay home, I was able to regain some of my strength without regret. The following journal entry, which I wrote after a heart-wrenching therapy session, is a perfect illustration of this pattern.

September 30, 2004

Tuesday morning I lay with ice packs on my eyes but determined to go to work. I believed I could not stay out. It was hell. I came home too exhausted to write/feel/do anything. Slept, got up, pushed to work. Driving there I called Dellene. I was so angry that I hadn't given myself a day to recover. My hands still hurt, I needed to cry, write, and rest. But I wouldn't turn around and go home. I felt such pressure to be at work. Wednesday evening Dellene called. I told her what I was feeling. I started to cry. She said, I never tell you what you need to do. I'm telling you now you need to stay home. We talked awhile and I agreed to stay home.

Remember, it is okay not to be okay. It is okay to let someone take care of you. And, most important, it is more than okay to take care of yourself. You're worth it!

The workplace is often a stable, predictable part of life. During the days and hours when you are there, you can count on using the time as a respite.

Creating a Respite

The need to create a temporary place of respite occurs when you aren't working. Evenings, weekends, and vacations—times most people treasure—can become unbearable if you're physically and emotionally consumed by the pain surrounding abuse. For those who are unemployed, the need for respite has a meaning all its own. The potential exists to become trapped in your surroundings at home, never escaping from the pain of abuse. The question becomes, where and how do you create this needed space? Think of it as a shelter made just for you. What does that shelter need to look like? What must be inside and surrounding it to help you relax? As with the workplace, the location must be engineered by you, the conductor. The goal is to let your mind escape from its ever-churning thoughts and to grant yourself a short period of time when your mind and body can be at rest. Sometimes this means creating a void—a pause in time when you can wrap your mind and body in something soft, empty yourself of thought altogether, and produce a temporary calm in the storm. There are three essential steps to take when creating this respite: construct the atmosphere, maintain a contact, and choose the location.

Only you can know the conditions that will create the ideal atmosphere for your respite, but the right physical attributes often help achieve it. It is your job to be sure they're in place. A warm blanket, candlelight, and soft music are all elements that might help you to create a special location in which to experience rewarding periods of rest. If you are creating this respite at home, let those around you know that you need some quiet time—no phone calls, questions, or interruptions.

Maintaining a contact means letting someone know you're seeking a respite and where you will be. If possible, have someone with you—someone whom you trust and who already knows your plight. (I chose either my husband or my friend Nancy to support me during my own respites.) Then plan how long you'll be gone. It makes no sense to get away only to be worrying if you will get back in time for your children, your pets, or some other responsibility. Setting a time to return will alleviate unneeded stress. If you choose to leave home

60

alone to find your respite, have a cell phone with you. Let someone know where you are and how long you will be away. Victims of abuse and particularly victims doing the work of healing are fragile. We need control and privacy, yet we must be prepared for those times when our emotions take over and we need someone else to take control for us. By maintaining a contact, you are assuring your safety during your time of respite.

Your options for choosing a location of respite are limitless. Finding this room in your home allows you to avoid having to drive, but sometimes home is not conducive to becoming a place of respite. If you need quiet space elsewhere, a park or a church may provide the atmosphere you need. A shopping mall or movie theater can work if you need your mind to be distracted. The choice is yours, and it will change depending on your needs at the time. The only right location is the one that will provide a respite from the work and pain that lead to healing.

The home Tim and I share is a geodesic dome. As such, it is very open and doesn't provide many quiet places to find personal space. Our bedroom is a place of retreat, but not one of respite. During my healing journey, it was the first place I'd go to be alone, to cry, to rest and recover from the hardest days. It was where I experienced nightmares, where I went when I was in the depths of sadness, and where I wrote in my journal. For all of these reasons, it could never be my place of respite.

At some point I decided that my living room—a peaceful, sunlit room—would never be associated with my healing work. If I was on the phone with my therapist, I wouldn't sit in that room. In the early stages, when I was still conversing with Clara, we would not sit in the living room. In these ways, I managed to keep one place in my home untainted by the pain of abuse. As a result, I often found calmness in my living room: lighting candles and playing a relaxing CD, reading, or just sitting and staring, clearing my mind of the noise that clamored within. Sometimes I'd wrap myself in an afghan and take a nap. On a quiet day, these activities were my respite for an hour or so.

When our children were home, no part of the house was conducive to being a place of respite, so I needed to change the location. If I decided to have someone with me, a specific destination didn't matter. Sometimes a short drive was enough. As the passenger, I could enjoy the scenery or just stare out the window. Most of the time I preferred not to engage in conversation. I constructed the atmosphere by stating my need for quiet. There were other times when I wanted to be by the water. A beach in the off-season, where I could listen to the waves and gulls, was a perfect setting. Still other times I found solace in an empty church. These environments all became temporary respites that allowed me to clear my mind, relax, and rebuild my energy.

There will be times during your healing journey when your emotions will be too intense for you to reach this level of relaxation. What then? How do you create a much-needed time of respite when your mind is racing? It will take some extra effort, but it is possible. Instead of trying to empty your mind, try to replace your raging thoughts with less meaningful ones, such as by finding a focus of interest that will be temporarily stronger than your focus on yourself. One example is to go to or rent a movie. It is possible to immerse yourself in someone else's drama, even fictional. A television show can serve the same purpose. During my six years of therapy, I became an expert at solving episodes of *Law & Order*.

Another idea is to allow yourself time to do something you normally enjoy. Doing so was always a concerted effort for me—I had little or no energy for hobbies—but on the days when I was able to force myself to give a sewing project some attention or create a meal, the outcome was positive: I'd lose myself in the process. The basis of this idea is permission to concentrate on something other than your pain and thereby create a natural time of respite. For me, making new curtains or chopping ingredients to precise size became a fixation that did not leave room for the thoughts of a victim. At times I hyperfocused and the task took on an exaggerated importance; however, if the time I spent sewing or cooking freed me of an hour of anxiety or emotional pain, then it served a worthy purpose on the days when nothing else would work.

Summary

Using your workplace as a distraction, creating a quiet place to empty your mind, or focusing on a task intensely enough to push thoughts aside are all ways to free yourself from your journey for the moment. A respite is a necessity. You cannot "run on empty" for long. Sometimes the slightest break is all you need to renew your energy. Remember, you're trying to survive one day at a time. If you can get through a day with the energy to face the next, you've accomplished a goal—and one more step toward healing.

5
Journaling

Journaling is the process of writing your thoughts and experiences on paper and can be a beneficial strategy throughout therapy. You might question the validity of keeping a journal during this tumultuous time in your life. One reason for doing so is comfort. The word itself, *journaling*, offers a calming effect—flowing, soaring, a gentle motion, a movement forward, a journey with words.

Two weeks into my therapy, Dellene suggested journaling as a means of releasing my feelings. I have since filled six journals. They represent my past and chronicle how I arrived at this state of healing. They tell the story of revolving emotions: the steep climbs to great heights where I experienced a blanket of peace, the spiraling lows that left me with little hope, and the endless days void of any emotion. Each entry reflects a deeply personal view of my journey. My courage to expose myself by sharing these writings in such a public way comes from my fervent hope that others will see the value in taking the journey toward healing.

When keeping a journal, you'll want to consider a few priorities. The first is the location where you write. Just as with creating a respite, a quiet, comfortable setting, free from interruptions, is essential to journaling. If there are others in your home, let them know you need time alone. If possible, turn off your phone while writing. Choose a place you find relaxing. I often wrote in my bedroom with a candle lit and soft music playing. Safety is the next journaling-related priority to consider. Sometimes I preferred being outside, at a park or near the water. Whatever your location, it is important that you are safe there. Because the outcome of your writing is unpredictable and has the potential to raise extreme feelings of sadness or anger, it is important to have someone nearby and aware that you are journaling. Following a journaling session, you may need to talk about the experience and be assured you're not alone and that you are safe.

A final priority for me was the journal itself. I chose one with lined pages that I received at a retreat. On the light-green cover are the words WOMEN OF FAITH. I was fortunate to find identical new journals as I filled the previous ones. You may wish to buy multiple copies of the same journal if you find it has meaning for you.

The Benefits of Journaling

A journal provides:

- a private place to express feelings and thoughts you aren't ready to say out loud
- a place to document new insights you will access later
- a safe place to release anger, pain, and sadness
- a place to write words of consolation, support, and hope
- an ongoing chronicle of your journey to healing and a validation of how far you've come

There are no restrictions on how or what you write in a journal. Your purpose for writing will vary depending on your needs at the time, and the end of a journal entry may look very different from its beginning. That doesn't matter. What matters is that you let uncensored feelings flow. You're not writing for anyone's eyes but yours. No words are too harsh, too sad, too honest, or too angry. Capitalization, punctuation, and spelling have a purpose only if they serve a purpose for you. They are your words, your feelings. Remember that there is no right or wrong. As you move through the process, the visual appearance of your writing will change but the benefits of the journal will remain the same: it's a place to unveil private thoughts, new insights, emotions, and expressions of hope while preserving your journey to healing.

There are two types of journal entries: the writing of facts and the writing of feelings. Most times, the two become intertwined. I will separate my examples of each for clarity, but it is rare that they do not both appear in one journal entry.

Journaling Facts

Writing a factual account following a therapy session serves two important purposes. The first is to revisit valuable ideas that emerge during a session. Whenever possible, I would write within hours of coming home from a therapy session. These entries often began, *Today we talked about . . .* and included an "I said, she said" account of the session. Whatever was significant about the week, I put on paper before I forgot it. If I needed to refer to those thoughts during the week, I had a simple way to retrieve them.

September 25, 2001

I had my session and we touched on a lot. Mostly my need to express my anger—do it in little bits, do something physical while letting it out, I'm turning that anger inward. I doubt everything about myself again. I'm depressed, tired, worn out. It takes energy to suppress anger. My guard is up and when I let it down I feel so depressed, I feel like I don't want to go on. Dellene said when I was young if I let my guard down I was not safe. Now again if I let my guard down I am not safe. I need to start spending time alone again. Writing, thinking, listening to music. Let myself feel. I have to work on anger, my fear (which I did not tell anyone) I will start beating on myself—physically. I hope not but it seems like it would feel good and I have to face that and be honest about it.

This entry reminded me that I needed to work on my anger in a constructive way. My therapist helped me to understand why I kept my guard up. Putting the thoughts in my journal helped me to realize I was not in the place of that little girl; I was safe. I also understood, at least for the time being, that suppressing anger and turning it inward drained me of my energy and strength to go on doing the work I so needed to do.

Writing following a session provided a time to reflect. It became especially important when I needed to work further on an issue. Your mind is flooded with thoughts and emotions. Your body often reacts to the stress from getting too little sleep. Ideas from a session that you wish to continue working on may be difficult to recall days later. Often as I wrote about a session, I became aware of a significant concern. Writing afforded me more time to think, dissect, and process my thoughts surrounding that concept. If I knew I needed to spend more time on those thoughts at my next session, I made a note of it. Before I returned to Dellene's office, I would reread what I had written so that it would be fresh in my mind.

July 26, 2004

I just came from my appointment and don't want to forget an important point to continue discussing. Over vacation I had a few bad days. First night I had a dream of someone jumping out in the dark and scaring me. Second night I was in the house—in high school, nighttime—Rune at the kitchen door drunk, trying to get in, naked, coming around to the hatchway door. Me telling him how much he disgusted me. For about three days I was quiet, pulled away from Tim. We talked—talked all about it—but I was anxious and as Tim thought trying to anticipate everything. Really I was needing to be in control. Also I was upset, crying—I want this over, behind me. I don't want to feel this way. I reflected a lot on how sick and sad the past has been and how much it affected the kids and our family structure. It was all upsetting to me. I realized I don't want to accept that this was my life, this is a part of me—it's not just going to be "over."

I shared all of this with Dellene. She mentioned the control thing and also me being hard on myself. I worked through all of this. I'm better. Why didn't I have control to stop that dream? What I need to remember and talk about is my need to accept this as my life—not an event that happens and then is over. But also—when that happened over vacation, it gave me an angry feeling that this is going to taint my life forever. It's never going to be "good." The filth will keep invading. I will end up an old lady sitting alone in my kitchen, having gone nowhere—life ruined, tainted forever because of them. This I have to deal with. I have to come to an understanding that it was filth—it did harm me but didn't ruin me. I have to believe I can maintain mental health. That I will rise above. I need to talk this through more. I will.

The most significant part of this entry came at the end: what happened in my life did not ruin me. It was a new thought I needed to explore with my therapist. I went back and read this entry before my next appointment.

It is also helpful to journal between therapy sessions. You may want to write about something someone said to you that raised an emotion or a new insight into your past. A question for your therapist may come to mind. At times a thought might arise that you don't want to explore alone or lose track of.

I wrote the following journal entry when I discovered Clara's involvement in my abuse. The memories were far too painful and frightening to work through alone. Just putting these thoughts into written words gave the thoughts life and meant I would not be able to hide from them. I'd now have to do the work, but only in the right setting, at the right time.

April 22, 2002

I live so much inside of myself. The closest people don't know what I live with day after day. It's okay, they couldn't possibly know. It's hard though. I guess it can't be any different. There is a hollow loneliness to this pain. He (Rune) will never know what he did to me. She (Clara) too will never know but for her it's her choice. She should be by my side, holding me, helping me, supporting me, loving me. She is my biological mother only. In no other way is she a mother to me. I'm not dealing with this now. It's work I can do only with Dellene. Never alone.

It wasn't unusual for me to scan through my journal before a session to reread an entry exactly like this. By doing so, I was putting myself on notice. It is much easier to go into a session saying, "I don't really have any pressing issues this week." But easy is not what we want. What we want is to heal and to heal means doing the work. Keeping track of the hard issues helps to keep the process in motion. It is nearly impossible to ignore your own written word. In a sense, you have said it out loud.

Journaling Dreams

Journaling dreams and memories is a way to maintain control over thoughts that could become destructive if you try to suppress them. When I relived a memory or incident of abuse during therapy, I needed to write about those sessions to preserve their intensity and the effect they had on my healing process. As you will read in chapter 6, "Visualization," these sessions were the most difficult and most powerful for me. Documenting them put them to rest. The memories are out, over, and on paper. They will not happen again. I can revisit them if I need to or never read them. The choice is mine.

I wrote the following journal entry after a session in which I revisited one of my many incidents of abuse. In the days leading up to this session, I had recurring dreams and thoughts about the bathroom in my childhood home. I did not want to remember what happened there, but the anxiety was destroying me. I wrote in my journal about wanting to vomit my insides out and scream away the terror. When I next met with Dellene, I knew I had to visually go back to that bathroom and release the memory.

May 27, 2002

"Close your eyes, breathe into it, don't force any thoughts, see what comes up" were Dellene's words. For a while I felt myself gripping my hands tighter and tighter, then rocking my foot. All of a sudden I slapped my hands over my face and it started— I was a little girl standing by the sink, Clara scrubbing me

clean with a washcloth. It hurt already and now it hurt more. Scrubbing, clean pj's, back to bed. Nothing mattered to her as long as I was clean. I cried and cried—maybe this time she'll take me in my room and hold me. Don't you want to hold me?

Following that night, I had many more memories of Clara's involvement and the emotional pain she caused. I could face each one only in small increments, but by recording them in my journal, I was able to regain the strength I needed to move forward.

I was also plagued by nightmares during my first year of therapy. For those of you who vividly remember dreams, like I do, the fear or disgust can linger long after you've awakened. When I began the following journal entry, it occurred to me that I had a strategy to release my fear and allow me to rest.

February 22, 2001

It's 5:00 AM. I'm awake from another dream. I can't close my eyes. Maybe if I write it, it will be out of me . . .
I wrote it. So now maybe I can close my eyes.

The nightmare was tucked into the pages of a journal. It could no longer hurt or terrify me. Writing it down also allowed me to put the dream aside until I was ready to deal with it in the proper setting, with my therapist.

Most of us have to go on with our jobs and family lives. We can't always confront difficult issues at the moment they arise. Keeping them on the surface makes it nearly impossible to function. Writing things down will allow you to make it through your day while preserving the important issues you'll discuss when the time is right.

During my therapy sessions, I did most of the talking. However, some of the insights Dellene provided throughout our work became my saving graces. I'd write her words in my journal and often mark the pages where they were written. During the week, when I needed something to hold on to—emotional support, a reason to keep going—I'd reread her comments. I've read them so many times by now that they have become etched in my mind. There are too many to put them all into this book, and you will find your own quotes that will become saving graces, but the following are a few of my favorites:

- You already survived the abuse; you can survive this.

- Don't force the thoughts; you will know all you need to know in time.

- You couldn't handle this if it all came rushing back at once.

- Listen to your body, rest, take a hot shower, breathe slowly and deeply.

- The fear is the fear you were never able to express as a child.

- Change the thought.

- Hurting yourself is giving them the power to hurt you again.

- It happened then; it is not happening now. These are just the feelings the child was never allowed to express.

- There is a core in you that they did not destroy.

- There are no right or wrong feelings; they are just your feelings.

- Hope dies hard.

- Give yourself permission to put the thought aside, knowing we will deal with it later.

Whether it is your therapist, a friend, or a loved one, if someone offers words of wisdom and you find them helpful, write them down. The times you need to hear the words again will be the times when you are too distraught to remember them. Referring to your journal and rereading the words then will offer comfort. I often compared the process to using a life jacket. When I was going down, I would reach for the thoughts that could keep me afloat.

Journaling Feelings

I think of the process of journaling feelings as a continuum from a gentle summer breeze to a winter's tempest winds. Feelings emerge and grow in intensity throughout the journey to healing. Journaling about a feeling, journaling about the feelings associated with an event, and journaling as a release of raw emotions can be powerful tools in the therapeutic process.

Some days, you'll write consciously about a feeling. These entries have structure and purpose. They're about your feelings, not about a release thereof. You're able to maintain control and logical thought while you are writing. This type of writing is reflective and will often help you to understand the emotional changes you're experiencing. In the following journal entry, I describe my tumultuous feelings as if I were documenting a reflection in a mirror, and evaluate my internal conflict of life versus death as stoically as someone deciding which coat to wear.

October 1, 2001

October 3 it will be ten months since I started therapy and in some ways I think I'm at my lowest point. No one, except possibly Dellene, would guess that. I'm in constant internal turmoil. Even when I'm good on the outside I'm questioning what is good about a constant pit in my stomach, tight shoulders, pain. I am always on the edge of wanting to give up. I feel so alone. I can't express myself to anyone. I'm in so much pain. I am like two people. One doesn't want to go on, one is a fighter; one is deep within me, unable to share, one is open to those who love me; one is near death, one is near life. Who will win?

As distraught as I was during this time, this entry simply stated my feelings. Doing so allowed me to acknowledge the conflict and pain I lived with every day, without experiencing the emotion.

Nightmares, uncomfortable social situations, and media exposure of sexual abuse are just some of the events that can trigger unwanted feelings. If you are journaling the facts of such an event, the feelings are sure to seep in. When I was journaling about a nightmare, I often wrote about my physical symptoms, including waking in a sweat with my heart pounding. I acknowledged the feeling of being too afraid to get out of bed, needing to wake my husband, and wanting to turn on a light. Writing my reaction to the nightmare not only helped to ease the discomfort but also led me to realize the unspoken fears I had as a child.

Releasing feelings in writing is the most intense use of journaling. When I look back on these kinds of journal entries that I wrote, I realize that I worked so hard at containing the emotions that the beginning of the entry was often calculated. But I couldn't maintain that level of control, because the feelings were too strong and ready to explode out of me. My pen couldn't move fast enough. Handwriting and sentence structure melded into a blur of illegible words. The force of my pen sometimes embedded words on the pages. At times, pictures or deep slashes that ripped through the page replaced the words altogether. I wrote the following journal entry on a Sunday prior to a Thursday meeting with Clara, Clara's therapist, and Dellene; it is a perfect example of my emotions taking off like a runaway train.

July 28, 2002

In preparation for Thursday, I've been going through my journals. I've approached this as if I'm prepping for a workshop presentation, doing research and making notes. I'm getting more and more upset as I go on. This journal is number four. I'm almost halfway through it. The first journal is primarily about him. From there on guess who's the reoccurring demon? HER! Have I been blind? Am I an idiot? What is my fear of confronting her? Page after page of ways that she hurt me then and now. Over and over!

The intensity of my feelings increased to a point where I could no longer write—I could only release. I later wrote that I threw a book against the wall, ripped out its pages, rocked, and sobbed. But because I was in the safety of our home, with Tim aware that I was journaling, I was safe. Once he detected that I was in distress, he intervened by encouraging me to take the antianxiety medication my doctor had prescribed me and by holding me in his arms until I fell asleep.

Writing an entry that led to this degree of emotional release always left me drained of energy. At times I felt vulnerable, at other times a bit afraid. If you encounter these feelings, be aware that they are normal. Allow your body and mind the time they need to recover. Rest, let someone take care of you, have a warm beverage. If you have been prescribed medication to help you relax, this would be a good time to take it.

Containing strong emotions is exhausting. Releasing them is equally exhausting, but the reward is the tranquility that follows. A bit of destructive anger, pain, or sadness has been cleansed away. The feelings will resurface, but the moments of peace afterward will give you renewed strength. Facing the pain and anger brings you closer to your goal of healing. Yes, it is difficult, and yes, you can do it!

The next journal entry does not fall under the heading of "Facts" or "Feelings" but rather "Prayers." As I ended a journal entry, there were times when I wanted to write a prayer. If you do not believe in God or pray to some higher power, you may wish to use this space to write positive statements. Writing prayers was an opportunity for me to reflect on my blessings—the people who were by my side throughout this process. It was also a time to ask for strength, as I knew it took every bit I had to go on. The following are some of those special words.

Dear Lord, please bring me peace. Please let me know that I am not making this up. I'm not mentally ill. Please take the fear away. He's dead and he will not ever touch me again, torture me. Lord, help me through. Let the door open. Let the flood happen. I will survive. I am stronger than he ever was. I will survive. Lord, be with me. Lord, be with Tim. I need him.

God, please give an extra blessing to Tim and Dellene today. They are my saviors, they will give me life. I was asked if I resent you, Lord. No, never. It was your hand that held mine, that made me survive, that made me strong. Please don't let go now. I need your strength.

I pray for peaceful sleep tonight and I thank God for Tim and Dellene. I will make it because I am a survivor.

The benefits of journaling extend even beyond these examples. Once you are well on your way to healing, life will look brighter. There will be more and more consecutive days when you feel happy and enjoy yourself. Your mind will allow you to let go of your darkest days and focus on the positive outcome of your hard work. I often compare this experience to childbirth: How often has a woman said she forgets the pain of giving birth the moment her baby is placed in her arms?

As much as your increasing ability to experience joy and wholeness will be a blessing, you can still find value in rereading portions of your journals. For me, doing so is an affirmation of my strength and a validation that I can accomplish anything because I have already accomplished the grueling task of facing my demons. My journals are a reminder of how fortunate I am to be living the life I cherish today.

Summary

Journaling gives you a private venue to express, release, and document your experiences. I suggest journaling facts following and between therapy sessions and as a means of storing memories and dreams. Journaling can also focus on a specific feeling, on feelings associated with an event, or on a more intense release of emotions. Yet another comforting way to use a journal is to write prayers or positive statements in it.

6
Visualization

Visualization requires some understanding and a great deal of trust. The person who is visualizing must believe they have the power to create a mental image that will provide a temporary refuge from fear, anxiety, or even a person. If you're skeptical, I still encourage you to try visualization. I will explain the process and share my experiences with this technique, and you will know after a few attempts if it is right for you by whether you find relief in that refuge or continue to experience discomfort.

To visualize means to form or create a mental image of something. Visualization became a powerful strategy in my therapy—to create distance, to create a barrier between myself and another person, and to re-create memories. Visualization is not an automatic response to a situation; rather, it must be consciously contrived. The conditions have to be right, and you are the only one who can know what those conditions are. This is particularly important if you are using visualization in a therapy session or with another person present. It is imperative that you speak up and say what is essential for you to feel comfortable. There's no room for guesswork on your therapist's part or discomfort on your part when you engage in visualization. The more you use the technique, the easier it will be to identify the right conditions. They are founded in personal preference and influenced by individual encounters with abuse, but I hope that in sharing my own experience, I will give you insight into what your own preferences would be.

Early in my treatment, I realized that the setting for my visualization sessions could have a positive or negative impact on my ability to relax and focus on the work I needed to do. Two conditions were directly related to the environment surrounding incidents of my abuse. The first was the lighting in the room. If the lighting was too bright, I felt exposed. I could neither relax nor close my eyes and visualize. As a child, I felt embarrassed and shamed by having to see a naked male body, as well as by having my body exposed in the brightness of the bathroom light, so I could not expose my thoughts, memories, or feelings in a bright room during therapy. Telling my therapist and turning on a small, softer lamp made all the difference.

My second condition was background noise—more difficult to control but as important as lighting. I remember one occasion when Dellene and I met in a different room for a therapy session. In this room, the blower for the heating system made a soft but constant noise. Its steady hum caused me to become anxious and unable to relax and focus. What was the connection? In my childhood bedroom, I had a window fan. In those days, fans were not quiet. I used to lie in bed at night, listening for my father's footsteps, but the continuous droning of the fan's motor made it difficult for me to hear him on his way to my room. The memory of that anxious feeling prevented me from being able to clear my mind and focus on the task of visualizing.

We've already discussed the importance of developing a relationship of trust with your therapist. That level of trust is crucial to visualization's success as a strategy in therapy.

Visualization to Create Distance

Creating distance is a good place to begin using visualization as a therapeutic technique, as it requires the smallest amount of emotional energy. As I look back on my years in therapy, I see how using visualization to create distance acted as a practice session for bigger things. I'll provide three examples of using visualization to create distance: distance from conversations, distance from feelings, and distance from dreams. Use these as a catalyst for exploring other situations when visualization would work for you individually.

There will be times when you will feel ready to share information about your healing journey with others. It could be a family member or friend with whom you choose to share; it may be a priest, minister, or rabbi from whom you are seeking support; it may be a boss or coworker who needs to know you're going through a difficult period. Most likely, time will lapse between your making the decision to talk with this person and the actual conversation. The thought of this discussion can be all-consuming, even as you continue to function in your everyday life at work and with your family. Anxiety will likely set in as you rehearse the conversation in your mind; you'll perseverate on what you will say and how the person might respond.

How can you use visualization to get you through the days until the conversation happens? Find a quiet place where you can close your eyes. Envision the conversation as a script. Put the script in a box, and imagine putting that box in a safe place. Once you do so, you will be less likely to obsess on the thoughts surrounding that conversation and more able to move on with your life until the day of your meeting.

In chapter 3, "Relationships," I talked about a situation that prompted me to tell a friend what I was dealing with prior to an overnight visit. The thought of having that conversation made me anxious. What if she thought I was crazy or, worse, didn't believe me? What if she couldn't be supportive? How would I feel? I chose my closest childhood friend to confide in. As young girls, we spent most of our time together; I loved going to her house, a safe place. As adults, we remained close, though we saw each other only a few times each year.

When I called her to say I needed to talk about something serious, we set a date for a few days later. The days in between left me immobilized. How would I start this conversation? What would I say? What would she say? Did she remember anything I had not recalled? Unlike my husband and my therapist, this person knew me during the years of my abuse. As surely as I knew the abuse happened, I feared hearing external confirmation of it.

In the interval before we met, I needed relief from my anxiety. No matter how many conversations I constructed, I couldn't predict what her reaction would be to hearing that Rune had sexually abused me. It was a perfect time to use visualization techniques.

In the quiet of my room—no interruptions, door shut—I closed my eyes and envisioned the room with her sitting across from me. I could see the warmth in her eyes and remembered why I called her my closest friend. I practiced saying the words I would use to tell her about Rune. As I imagined the two of us, I carefully took the picture in my mind and placed it in a safe, pretty box. I closed the lid and knew the vision and thoughts would stay there until we talked. My anticipation of our conversation came to mind over the next few days but no longer consumed me. I was free to face life's demands with a bit more energy.

Visualization to Create Distance from Feelings

Tightness in your stomach builds. Your throat dries. Anger or sadness takes over, but it isn't the time or place to express those feelings. Your body is poised to take on anyone who looks at you the wrong way. There's a risk you'll aim your anger at a coworker or a stranger. When you are not sure how to set those feelings aside, you may find that to be another opportune time to employ visualization. The process is much like visualizing distance from a conversation. A few minutes alone in a quiet room is all you need. Picture lifting those feelings out of your body and gently placing them in a box. Put that box in a safe place, with the understanding that you're merely putting the feelings on hold until you can find a time and place to release them in a healthy way.

My drive to work each day took about twenty minutes, enough time for my mind to wander and seethe. On several occasions, I found myself fighting back tears and too often crying with only a few minutes left in my commute. Knowing I could not go in to work in this state, I'd pull off to the side of the road. Within a few minutes, I'd create a mental image of a room. I would visualize lifting the emotions from within me, gently placing them in that room, and locking the door until the workday ended. This exercise helped me to regain control of the day. Those few extra minutes made the difference between my experiencing a successful day at work and needing to turn around and go home.

Visualization to Create Distance from Dreams

Yet another time visualization can be effective is when you have a bad dream. Dreams for the abused are more accurately described as nightmares. They come in the middle of the night, when your body is crying for a peaceful night's sleep, and they can leave you anywhere from confused to trembling with fear. It is dark, everyone else is asleep, and you are left to lie awake in your bed, afraid to fall back into the terrifying dream. Using visualization can help create the distance you need until you can deal with the nightmare in the light of day, in a safe setting and in the presence of someone you trust.

Sometimes I awoke confused, wondering if the circumstances of a particular dream were signs of what was to emerge in my conscious mind. There were very few details in these dreams, but the feelings that remained were unsettling. More often I awoke shaking, my heart pounding, sweating from raw fear. The ugly visions were the ferocious monsters of my abuse, waiting to surface. The words of the dream needed to be spoken, and the fears expressed.

I was fortunate to have my husband by my side—someone to hold me and assure me I was safe. Sometimes that was all I needed, but more often I needed to talk about the dream. The middle of the night wasn't the best time to do that—there's a difference between confronting fearful events in the daylight and trying to face them in the darkness. Still, I needed to actively do something that made me feel safe enough to fall asleep. Visualization helped. I'd close my eyes and create a vision of a box, this time with a lock. Scooping the dream into my hands, I'd visualize locking it in the box and leaving it there until daylight, when I was ready to put the dream into words.

Following one of my first nightmares, I wrote in my journal as an attempt to ease my fears. I was not yet experienced at using visualization as a strategy. The next morning, the dream still haunted me, and

I called my therapist. This journal entry from that day begins with Dellene's advice.

February 23, 2001

Get in bed under the covers—soft music, feel safe, close your eyes, put the words of the dream in a box, lock the box in a closet or somewhere, bring your mind to a peaceful place, stay there at least an hour, get up for a while and call me. If this didn't work I was to call her, go see her and talk out the dream, but she said it would be good if I could learn how to do this because it was most likely going to happen again.

It did happen again, many times, and yes, it was vitally important for me to learn how to take a dream, a fear, a feeling, and lock it away until the time was right.

Visualization will not change your experience or erase your emotions. What it will do is allow you the distance you need to get through a day or night. Think of it as taking the edge off or making life more bearable until you are ready and able to deal with the experience in an appropriate setting. Besides bringing some sense of relief, the act of visualization keeps *you* in control, rather than letting your thoughts, feelings, or dreams take control of you.

Visualization to Create a Barrier

The use of visualization for the purpose of separating from a person, rather than from a conversation, feeling, or dream, requires greater concentration and can be more difficult to achieve. But if the technique doesn't work the first time, don't give up; its value is worth a second try, whether you are creating a barrier around another person or creating a barrier around yourself.

Creating a Barrier Around Another Person

Creating a barrier around a person entails visualizing that person and putting them in a place that separates them from you. You are in complete control of where they are and when you'll let them out. As you will see, visualization becomes a means of protection, alleviating the daunting fear of their presence. For anyone who has been abused, the mere concept of being able to protect oneself is powerful. The best way to explain this process is by sharing the following two journal entries, in which I describe separating from one of my abusers by using visualization.

March 8, 2001

I've had such poor sleep. I'm more tired in the morning than when I go to bed. My stomach hurts—I can't focus. After much thought, I've decided it's that I'm fighting becoming aware of something. He is haunting me.

After I wrote that journal entry, I had a horrific nightmare involving Rune. In my dream I had assaulted him but he kept returning, standing before me, just staring at me.

March 9, 2001

The worst part of today is not the gross parts but him standing there all bandaged and clean and just staring at me. I had to call Dellene. She said I need to plan how I am going to put him away, lock him up—take control over him. Tell him he had control but doesn't now. Plan it and then do it. Make it a big event and don't be afraid to use the angry feelings I have to do it. Don't be nice—be as nice to him as he's been to me. Then try to relax, nap, and have a quiet night.

It can't be here on our property. It will be in the wine cellar of their house. With a dog—he feared dogs.

I dimmed the lights, lay on my bed, and set the scene. I visualized their cellar. The gray concrete floor, cleanly swept. To the left of the bottom stair was a small wine cellar with a wooden door and a metal latch. Canned goods filled the shelves on the right; a bag of onions, potatoes, and a gallon of homemade wine sat on the low shelf on the left. The room had one lightbulb, hanging from the ceiling. I envisioned Rune upstairs in the kitchen, sitting as he always did, with his legs crossed and a bottle of Ruppert Knickerbocker in his hand. I visualized grabbing him by the arm, throwing him down the cellar stairs, and pushing him into the wine cellar. I stripped him of his clothes. *I want you to feel as humiliated as I did!*

Before closing the door, I conjured the image of a dog, a big German shepherd, growling and baring his teeth. I sent the dog into the wine cellar. I imagined screaming, *Now you can feel some of the fear I felt from you!* I told Rune I'd let him out when I was ready to let him out. I slammed the door shut, nailed boards around the edges of the door, and left him there. I envisioned leaning against the door, relieved and safe. I lay still in my bed for a while, before opening my eyes. Calmness spread through my body. I was safe, free from him, for now.

The second example of creating a barrier around my abuser happened following a therapy session where I relived an incident that had occurred in the bathroom. I was shaken and unable to get the vision of the bathroom—his body, my fear—out of my mind. I needed to create a separation from Rune. The following is the journal entry I wrote that night.

June 2, 2001

The cellar won't work—it's a different him. The man in the cellar is old, sick. This man is young, healthy. Dellono suggests putting him in the tub facedown. There it is—perfect. I threw him in facedown—nailed on a top with a small opening. Filled it with burning hot water, leaving a few inches at the top. He can't die yet—I'm not done with him yet. Nail the bathroom door shut. Done!

I accomplished this task by closing my eyes and walking myself through the actions, first visualizing the bathroom: a small room with an old clawfoot tub, a sink, and a toilet. A little throw rug lay on the speckled linoleum floor. I envisioned complete control over

Rune as I threw him facedown into the tub. He was helpless against me. I nailed down the top and watched the steam rise as I filled the tub with scorching-hot water.

The visualization process was much easier this time, perhaps because I had more confidence that it would work. I succeeded at separating Rune and the scene in the bathroom, and that allowed me to function free from the fear and disgust surrounding those events.

On other occasions when my memories of abuse were bombarding me, I used visualization to protect me until I had the opportunity to deal with the memories at a therapy session. The following journal entry refers to a night at home when I began to remember that my abuse extended beyond my early childhood. It was a Monday night, and I was not scheduled to see Dellene until Wednesday. I was losing control and knew I could not face anything new unless I was in the safety of her office. The first step in taking control was to call her.

January 14, 2002

When Dellene called, I cried harder than I've ever cried—I can't do this! She assured me that I didn't have to do the work now—that I shouldn't. Get in the present—stay in the present. We talked about visualizing putting him away. I could do it. Be stronger than him. So once we hung up, I closed my eyes. Put him in the room of coffins at the funeral parlor. Tied his hands and feet, facedown, strapped his neck, nailed the box shut, carved PIG on the coffin. All set until I'm ready to deal!

Taking control and visualizing Rune locked up gave me power over my villain and control over my life until it was time to confront the new memories in the safety of my therapist's office.

Creating a Barrier Around Yourself

My final example of creating a barrier was so effective that I want to share it as a possibility for others. In essence, I created an imaginary barrier around myself. It was a time when memories flooded back, accompanied by intense emotional pain. Equally powerful were my thoughts of slipping away, losing control. The ugliness of my past was taking over. I had to do something to save myself.

The visualization exercises I did during this time took place in therapy. Rune's presence haunted me, as did my loneliness about having been an abandoned child. I questioned why no one protected me, why my mother left me to endure the horror, rather than stop him. Clara's only answer was that she didn't know Rune was abusing me. The pain gripped my insides. I had thoughts of giving up, thoughts of suicide. Some days I would lie on my bed and picture my family moving on without me. *Would they be better off?* I thought. Sadly, in those dark times, I wasn't sure of the answer. Visualization was one step toward helping me cope. I wrote the following journal entry after I first shared my thoughts with Dellene.

May 21, 2001

I didn't want to do this but I built a box—metal—around me. I said my feelings are so raw and painful I can't let anyone in. She said it's okay. I'm preparing for the next stage. She said I have to have total control. The box around me is total control. I'll only let in whom I choose and when. She said that was important right now.

I used the vision of a metal box around me several times during the next few months as a means of protection. On one occasion I drew the box, with me inside, in my journal.

I often wonder if I lived in that box as a child. Perhaps that's how I survived. I know the image of it helped me through the darkest times in my therapy.

No technique is too unusual if it helps you. If it works and is not harmful, it's what you need to do.

Visualization to Re-create a Memory

The process of reliving memories using visualization is the most difficult to experience and for that reason the most difficult to describe. It is necessary to understand the importance of this process in order to believe it can work. Survivors of abuse often try to minimize the actions that took place. It is not uncommon to believe you deserved what happened or were in some way to blame. These are unhealthy and unsuccessful ways to push aside the pain and anger associated with sexual abuse.

The reality is, whatever the nature of your abuse—whether it happened once or over time; whether the abuser was a stranger, a friend, or a relative—it was still abuse. No one deserves to be abused, and there is no such thing as abuse being "not so bad." It is *all* bad. It is all damaging to the victim. In our quest to protect ourselves, victims often repress the actual incident or incidents that occurred. "I don't want to remember" seems like reason enough to hide from the facts. But, in truth, the actions happened, so, whether they're in your conscious mind or held subconsciously, the memories are there. Once someone has been sexually abused, there is no taking it away.

One might ask, But isn't it better not to remember? Why relive the horror? Can't life go on without bringing back the fear and pain? My answer is emphatically *no*, for two reasons. First, look at the damage repressed memories cause, and second, consider the freedom that comes from reliving those memories. Even if you are able to bury, or deep-six, an act of abuse from your consciousness, it will most likely rear itself in some physical form: headaches, a tightness in your chest, or, as I experienced, a "glob" in the pit of your stomach.

If I could draw a picture of what the memories looked like sitting inside me, the picture would look something like this: a dark purplish-black, thick, and heavy glob with no form. It would have briars sticking out of it in random places, and it would sit in the pit of my stomach. At times it would just feel like a heaviness inside me, but the slightest scent or semblance of my abuser would cause the briars to scratch my insides, making me bleed. At the worst times, the glob would swell into my throat, making me feel as though I were choking.

The energy it took to suppress this "glob" drained me. Just when I had tricked myself into thinking life was good, an unexplained emptiness would overtake me. The best of times fell short of being fulfilling. An ever-present weight held me down. The guilt and shame that accompanied my abuse resulted in low self-esteem. I had difficulty making decisions and doubted the choices I did make. Even after I received a compliment, I would silently criticize my looks and actions. In my mind, I wasn't worthy.

For some, these repressed memories can be even more damaging. Many victims of sexual abuse become drug- or alcohol-dependent. Others live a life of prostitution or perpetuate the abuse by becoming abusers themselves. Whatever their degree, the damaging effects of repressed memories destroy the essence of life and the joy of being whole. Abuse never truly ends until you face the demons, release the memories, and free yourself to live the full life you deserve.

Think of reliving the memories as the act of seizing that glob and scraping every last bit of it out of you. It is an act of cleansing, of ridding yourself of the filth that works at destroying your life. By reliving the memories, you are releasing yourself from them. You are in control, saying they will no longer consume you. And once they are out, there's room for goodness, wholeness, and peace. Light replaces darkness. There are no words to describe the joy that comes from feeling whole when you've never experienced that joy before. Is it worth the pain of reliving the memories of abuse? It is life versus death, living in light versus living in darkness, knowing love versus not believing you can be loved. Yes, it is worth it, and it takes place in three steps: preparing, the process, and recuperating.

Preparing

Earlier in this chapter, I spoke of the right conditions for using visualization. It is critical at this stage, retrieving memories, to establish the conditions that make you feel comfortable and safe. Hopefully, if you are at this stage in therapy, your therapist will know some of the conditions that affect your ability to relax and focus. For me, the conditions were lighting and background noise. You'll also need to have complete trust in the person with you. You did not feel safe when the abuse happened, so it is important to feel safe now, when you are going to re-create a memory. No one is going to hurt you. You aren't being abused. You are remembering an incident from the past.

A final suggestion for setting the stage is to have a family member or friend available after the session. Revisiting the past means reliving the pain, anger, and fear that accompanied it. The experience is physically and emotionally draining, so driving afterward is unsafe. If I planned one of these sessions, my husband dropped me off. If it was unexpected, I would call him to pick me up. This meant leaving my car and getting it later, but it needed to be done.

Once you are home, it is wise to have someone there to take care of you. Most times I crawled into bed. I needed someone there to suggest I take my prescribed medication, make me a cup of tea, or just be by my side. This is not a time when you want to be alone. I was fortunate to have a supportive husband, but for others a sibling or trusted friend can serve the same purpose. The key word is *trust*. Remember, you will be vulnerable. Your deepest emotions will have been exposed. You will need to allow someone you trust to care for you until you are stronger.

The Process

So now you are prepared: your conditions are met, you have trust in your therapist, and someone is on call to care for you after the session. What happens next?

Unlike other sessions, where you choose a topic or feeling to discuss, you have much less control when you go back and relive the past. It will happen differently for each person, but there are some common threads among most survivors. Remembering an incident of abuse is not something we *want* to do. Therefore, it is going to happen out of need. For me, it always started with increased anxiety. Days would go by when my stomach muscles couldn't relax. The act of breathing seemed contrived. The anxiety would intensify to such a degree that I imagined I couldn't live within my own body. It was as if that "glob" were stuck in my throat, sometimes lasting a few days, sometimes a few weeks. This buildup always resulted in the same ending: I needed to face something—a memory fighting to come forth as I fought equally hard to suppress it.

Remembering the abuse is something any survivor would want to run from. Even later in my therapy, when I understood the positive outcome of releasing the horror, I still fought. I wouldn't for a minute try to lead anyone to believe that it isn't hard work. But each time I would endure it because I could no longer go on in that state. You might say I lost the fight but won the battle. Each time I relived a memory, I was that much closer to being healed and whole. One more bit of filth was out of me for good. The release and relief were well worth the hard work and pain.

Prior to revisiting an incident of abuse, I would experience the physical symptoms of suppressing a memory. I'd share these feelings with my therapist. She never pushed me forward but always said we would know when the time was right. Most often I'd walk into the office and say I couldn't go on like this any longer. Dellene would ask if I wanted to go back and see what was there. I never wanted to, but at that point I couldn't fight it. She would suggest I close my eyes and breathe deeply. Her quiet voice would say, "Relax. You are safe; you are not alone." I would attempt to block the thoughts. My leg would swing; I'd wring my hands or rock in my seat. But now it was too late—my thoughts traveled back to my bedroom, the bathroom, a place where Rune had committed his crimes.

At some point, the conscious thoughts would stop and I would visualize a black hole. As I emptied myself of thoughts, raw feelings would fill the space—sometimes gripping fear, sometimes emotional pain and tears, and other times rage. And then it would happen: I'd be in that place, reliving that memory that had been fighting its way out.

Sometimes it was as if I were watching a movie. The characters were Rune, sometimes Clara, and a young girl, me. On other occasions I was in that young body, seeing my abuser at work. I experienced the emotional and physical pain. The length of time would vary, but the vision always ended the same way: after a while, I would realize I was not in that horrific setting but in my therapist's office, safe and not alone. It would take time for me to feel secure enough to open my eyes. I often feared I would see Rune or Clara if I did open my eyes. Sometimes I'd ask if I was okay. The tears came from sadness for the little girl who endured that horror. Relief followed that sadness—relief at knowing the memory was out and the abuse was over. I now knew what had been building inside me and causing such intense anxiety. A blanket of calm wrapped my body.

Most times I needed to talk about the experience with Dellene, put words to the memory. It was also a critical time for me to hear that I was safe, I was okay, and I had done a great job. I often wanted to be held. Each experience of reliving the abuse was exhausting. It never got easier.

You may have times where you experience a set of your own symptoms leading up to reliving a memory, and even begin the process of deep breathing and feeling the physical reactions—and then nothing comes, nothing happens. It is important to realize that's okay. Perhaps you aren't ready to face the memory. Perhaps the timing or conditions aren't just right. Your only disappointment should be about the fact that you will have to live with the anxiety a few days or weeks longer. Never feel disappointed in yourself for not accomplishing the task. Your memories will unfold when you are ready and the time is right. Try to be patient.

The following journal entry is about the very first time I used visualization to remember my abuse—and the first time I recognized that Rune had actually raped me. A day or so after the session, I wrote what had happened.

May 30, 2001

*I'm not sure I can do this but I need to try. I'm home from school—
the first time I had to do that since I started therapy. It's been
five months and nineteen visits and I've come to where I knew I
had to go. After the last visit I was not well—nervous, blocking
emotion. A phone call to Dellene and Tim's intervention got me
to release more of the intense emotion of the visit. I sobbed and
felt better. Monday night it started again. Tim woke me because
I was whimpering in my sleep. I couldn't remember a dream but
never went back to sleep. My mind was racing—picturing the
bedroom, trying to piece something together. Two memories: 1)
the headboard with spindles and holding on so tight my hands
hurt, 2) crunching my body into the wall and crying. I never
slept and then got up for work. It was the first time ever that I
didn't want to see Dellene. I had a late 8:00 appointment. For
some reason I showered, put comfortable clothes on, and drove
slowly there. Sitting in the waiting room I prayed—another first.
I prayed for Dellene and myself that we could and would work
through this. I told God we were ready. All day and especially
after dinner I had a very real physical feeling. An ache in my
throat and stomach. When I went in I babbled about the weekend. Then I told her of this physical feeling—something stuck
inside of me. She asked if I wanted to go down and find out what
it was. Did I want to work this week? It was up to me. Yes, I can't
live with this feeling. It's different. It's not like when I am fighting
tears. It's really physically there. And now the real work began.
Take deep breaths, relax your body—go down inside and ask
yourself what is this pain, what's there, what am I feeling?*

*First nothing—then realizing my hands were clasped so tight
it hurt, then my whole body tensed. Deeper, darker—no, no, I
was afraid. Let it go, she said—it's okay. Let it go. No, no, no. Oh
God no—shaking, crying, a fear greater than I can imagine. On
my back, (Rune) foot of the bed—naked bottom, pajama top,
forcing my legs apart, forcing himself to enter. NO NO NO Oh
God no . . . that's it I can't bear any more—sobbing, coming back
up, out of myself, shaking. I don't want this to be true.*

The memory was so much harder and worse than I ever imagined. I told her I knew it was real from my feelings. No one could make up being that scared, feeling that much emotional pain, feeling so repulsed by someone. She asked if the physical feeling was gone—yes. I felt awful but better. When I realized I'd be telling Tim, I started to cry. I could barely ask but I asked if she could call him and tell him for me. She said yes and thought he should pick me up. I couldn't drive. While we waited for Tim to come she came and held my hands.

This was the first of many sessions where I used visualization as a tool to relive a memory. As I said, it never got easier, but knowing it would bring a sense of relief at least gave me the confidence I needed to go through the process.

Recuperating

Most times I took the next day off from work to recover from these sessions. Reliving abuse is emotionally draining and physically exhausting. It was not unusual for my hands, shoulders, legs, or whole body to ache after such an experience. It is important to allow yourself the time to emotionally and physically heal. The day after that particular session, I barely talked. I needed silence. I spent most days following a memory resting or sleeping—something I couldn't do after an incident of abuse. I was a child living a secret. No one rescued me. I survived by pretending nothing had happened. That's what the adults in my life did, so that's what I learned to do. Now it was time to provide the care the little girl never had. But that wasn't easy. I needed reminders from my husband and therapist that it was okay to take care of myself and to let others take care of me.

Once you are stronger, it is important to talk about the experience. I usually did so with Dellene within a few days of a session. We began these conversations by discussing how I had felt coming into the session and how I had fought going back in time and doing the work. It helped me to acknowledge my defenses and realize I had very little control once a memory began forcing its way out. It also helped to talk about my sense of relief once a memory had been exposed. As sad as the situation was, once the memory came forth, it was over. It could no longer haunt or hurt me. This had a very freeing effect. The more filth I released, the more room I had for joy and peace.

Talking about these experiences also gave me the opportunity to ask questions—questions for which I knew the answers but needed validation.

"Why do my hands ache so?" I would ask Dellene.

"You were wringing them the whole time," she would answer.

"Am I going to be okay?"

"You are going to be more than okay."

"It felt so real."

"You were letting the little girl feel what she felt and had to hide. It *was* real."

"I was scared."

"I know you were."

"I feel so sad."

"It *was* so sad."

"He was a bastard."

"Yes, he was a bastard."

"I'm exhausted."

"I have no doubt you are exhausted. It was hard work, and you did a great job."

As well as I knew the answers, I can still feel the comfort that came from hearing my therapist respond. Her words not only legitimized my experience but also brought calmness to a very unsettling time. It was the first time I had someone to talk to following an incident of abuse, and for the first time, someone listened! An incredible need that had never been met when I was a child had finally been fulfilled. What a powerful gift in the process toward healing. I cannot over-emphasize the importance of talking out the experience once you've relived a memory.

Summary

Visualization is a powerful tool in the process toward healing and becoming the person you want to be—a person who is whole. Without it, I would not have made it to this peaceful place. For therapists, I believe visualization techniques should be explained and encouraged; they can never be forced. For victims, I cannot stress enough the value of visualization. Whether you use it to create distance, create separation, or relive a memory, it helps. We can't fill our beings with joy and peace until we've rid ourselves of the filth of abuse.

Part III:
Living the Journey

"Living the Journey" explores how to meet the challenges that arise throughout the healing journey and the way changes in emotions affect everyday life.

7

Control

Throughout much of this book, I refer to control—knowing when to retain it and when to relinquish it—as one of the ground rules for implementing strategies. But the subject merits attention in and of itself. Survivors of sexual abuse harbor a need to be in control. This need is a direct outcome of their having been manipulated and stripped of control by their abuser. The feelings associated with a loss of control linger long after the abuse stops. Maintaining control becomes an important factor in the victim's ability to navigate through life. In the following journal entry, Dellene helps me understand my need for control.

March 21, 2001

With Dellene I admitted I've been edgy with Tim. I've needed to be in complete control. He can tell me the simplest thing and I'm annoyed. She said it's very normal to need control. I didn't have control for so many years of my life.

The need for control is normal. However, excessive control can be harmful. In this section, I will discuss the negative and positive levels of control and the importance of finding the right balance.

Some think of *control* as a synonym for *strength*. If you are in control, you are strong. Would that then mean that letting go of control is synonymous with weakness? I don't believe so. When I look back on my journey, the times when I was able to relinquish control and allow others to take care of me were the times when I exuded great strength. I did not allow my need for control to supersede what was best for my well-being.

I think of control as a regulator. There are some times when a high level of control is appropriate and other times when it is best to lower the control knob. Regulating one's level of control within a healthy range is the goal. I still haven't fully reached this goal—I, too, was a victim, violated and stripped of control. I am now a survivor, healed and whole, but that doesn't mean I have the ability to regulate my level of control, under control!

Clearly, regulating the need for control is one aspect of this work that is ongoing. The first step is to be aware that control is a distinct factor in your life. The next step is to understand the negative and positive levels of control. The final step is to find a healthy balance between the two.

Negative Level of Control

What is a negative level of control? When the control knob is set too high. A simple way to recognize control as a negative is when the need to control overrides what's best for your well-being. Negative levels of control can have a detrimental impact in three arenas: your workplace, your relationships, and your physical and emotional health.

Unless you own a one-person company, collaboration—the ability to discuss ideas and share responsibilities—is important in any work environment. Problem-solving skills are also necessary in many job settings. At the very least, an employee must be willing to follow the rules and directives of their employer. If you are unable to regulate your need for control, your performance at work can be compromised. It is easy to become that employee who always tries to get their own way, who shuns suggestions from others, and who resists any new initiative. You may become argumentative, not because you disagree but because an idea isn't your own, and your need to control your work environment can result in adverse relationships with coworkers. To an even more significant degree, an employee who is unwilling to comply with company rules might put their job in jeopardy for the sake of being in control; therefore, regulating this need may even mean the difference between being employed and being unemployed.

Healthy relationships also require a balance of control. Negative consequences can result from having too much, as well as too little, control. One definition of *relationship* is *a continuing attachment or association between persons.* Complete control is not *between* persons; it is *over* another person.

The control that victims can harbor stems not from a belief that they are always right or smarter, but from a fear of being dominated and ultimately hurt. Maintaining control provides a sense of security. Insecurity and fear in a relationship are generated by the abuser, not the partner in the relationship. Through therapy, the need for control can be put into perspective and regulated to a level that fosters a positive bond between two people.

In my marriage, I used to have a great need for control. Rarely did I blatantly take control, though; instead I would manipulate a situation until the outcome was my idea. If Tim thought I would benefit from a weekend getaway, I would oppose the idea, not because I didn't want to go, but because he was deciding what was good for me. His logic was hard to dispute, so, as a means of regaining control, I would respond with something like this: "Fine, we can go. I'll just have to grocery-shop right after work and stay up late tonight to get the laundry done. I'm exhausted, but I'll do it."

Many times after this retort, he would give up trying to convince me and we would stay home. If things didn't go my way, I would become agitated, silently stewing about feeling dominated. I know now that this underlying need for control was not fair to my husband or to our marriage, but not until I was well into therapy did I recognize and work on the issue.

On the other extreme, exerting little or no control in a relationship is also damaging. A low level of control is directly related to low self-esteem. Many victims lack the confidence to voice their opinions or make decisions when others are involved. The person who always responds, "Oh, you decide," or "Anything is fine with me," to the question "What do you want to do?" or "Where would you like to go?" may be construed as congenial. In truth, that person might not want to take control of the situation because they feel unworthy.

Always being the one to agree to a partner's decisions is unhealthy for the relationship. The most damaging effect of relinquishing control occurs when the victim is taken advantage of. Sadly, there are people who will befriend someone because they know they can have the upper hand. Whether it is to borrow money, complete a job, or serve a need, the victim with little control becomes an easy target.

A high level of control damages the very essence of what a relationship is meant to be: a continuing attachment or association between persons. A low level of control creates the risk for being taken advantage of and being victimized again.

A high level of control can become a source of physical and emotional self-destruction and can cause you to lose sight of what's best for you. Living with the control knob on high impedes your willingness to let others care for you or guide you to making healthy decisions. As I have mentioned many times throughout this book, there are situations when it is important to allow others to be in control for you. When your mind is clouded with anxiety, fear, and sadness or you are drained of all energy, it is time to let go of control and let others step in. If you are willing to listen to their suggestions, you can still maintain a level of control: the ideas are someone else's, but the choice to act on them is yours.

Throughout most of my therapy, I had difficulty accepting this concept. Whether someone suggested I stay home and rest, take medication, or call my therapist, if it wasn't my idea, I opposed it. I can still remember the tightness in my stomach as I dug my heels in to maintain control: "I can't stay home"; "I have a meeting today"; "I am not taking medication—I don't need it"; "I just talked to Dellene yesterday. I can't bother her again today."

I wrote the following journal entry the day after a session in which I relived a memory of Clara's coming into my room after Rune had abused me, not to comfort me but to tell me to go to sleep. I was devastated recalling that she was there and did not protect me.

October 24, 2001

I don't want to believe this. I opened my eyes and Dellene was as wonderful as other times, came and sat with me. She reinforced my feelings of how awful this was. She went and got Tim and she filled him in. He knew it was coming. She said I would feel exhausted and sad in the next few days. I feel numb today toward Clara and emotionally traumatized. Tim and Dellene felt I should stay home today and I fought the idea. When I got home I felt tired but good—a release of pain. This morning I felt awful, sore, exhausted, drained, decided I couldn't go to work. It was a good decision.

What I didn't include in the journal was my anger that night when Dellene and Tim suggested I stay home. I never wanted to let my work in therapy interfere with my work at school. They knew it was not in my best interest to go to work the next morning, and they were right, but at the time I needed to be in control. By morning I was able to accept their suggestion, and because it was my choice, I didn't feel stripped of control. Listening to the recommendations of those you trust is not losing control—it is making a healthy choice.

A final example of control affecting your personal well-being relates to eating. Many victims of abuse develop eating disorders. Anxiety often results in a victim's either being unable to eat or overeating; poor eating habits can also be a manifestation of control issues.

I wrote the following journal entry after a session three months into my therapy.

April 11, 2001

The last thing was eating. It came up that many abused women have eating disorders. I told her about my daily lunch, getting on the scale daily, watching what I eat. She said it's all about control.

I controlled everything I ate and checked the scale daily to see the pounds slipping away. A small yogurt, a piece of fruit, and a few fat-free saltines were my lunch for years. I allowed myself a sweet treat, but it was only one Hershey's kiss or one small square of a chocolate bar per day. I consciously kept my dinner portions small and rarely finished the food on my plate. It became emotionally satisfying but physically damaging. Although I was not anorexic, I was at an unhealthy weight that made me more susceptible to illness and diminished my energy.

Almost a year later, I still had thoughts about controlling my weight. I had been taking medication for anxiety. Although I wrote in the following journal entry that it helped with the anxiety, my biggest concern was weight gain as a side effect of the medication.

January 6, 2002

I decided to stop the medication. This morning I got on the scale—gained seven lbs. (Side effect of meds: increased appetite and weight gain.) I can't tell anyone how much that bothers me. I have to maintain control of my weight. Sometimes it's all I've got. I'm glad I stopped. I've exercised for four days and I'll watch what I eat. I know intellectually this is wrong. I'm thin—but when I gain I feel worse. I can't look in the mirror and see a big ass. How often did I hear I had a big ass! God I hate him.

For many reasons, my decision to stop taking the medication was a poor choice, the most important reason being that any patient planning a change in medication should discuss it with a doctor first. But because the extra weight turned on the "old tapes" in my head of words I heard over and over from Clara and Rune—*I was the big one; I had a big ass*—controlling my weight by going off my medication made me feel like I had power over my abusers. The downside was that my need for control overrode my need to address the anxiety that compromised my physical and emotional state. The right decision would have been to discuss medication options with my doctor and focus on exercise and a healthy diet.

Positive Level of Control

Now that we have looked at the negatives, what level of control can be deemed positive? Three strategies that all employ a positive level of control and promote personal well-being are to say no, to keep safe, and to be an advocate. Survivors can use these strategies both while healing and throughout their life beyond.

There's a connection between being a survivor of sexual abuse and having low self-esteem; along with poor self-esteem comes an aversion to using the word *no*. We're the people who join every committee, bake for every bake sale, and do the work of three people because we can't say no. *Yes* becomes our automatic response, without our giving thought to the price of taking on another task. Added responsibilities often lead to added stress and exhaustion, something we already have to cope with on this journey.

This is a time in your life when being attentive to your own needs is paramount. Being in control allows you to assess your situation before responding to a request. If you are too busy or stressed or simply don't feel up to the task, it is okay to say no and to thereby contribute to your own well-being.

Sometimes you will find it is in your best interest to say no to social invitations. The subject matter of a movie, the people attending an event, or the timing of a night out are all factors to consider. If something or someone makes you uneasy or reminds you of any aspect of your abuse, you need to decline the invitation. By taking control and saying no, you are protecting yourself from unneeded discomfort or emotional stress. Positive control equates with making good choices.

Most victims of abuse experience a heightened sense of fear and a need to feel safe. It is possible to take control of many situations in ways that will result in your feeling more secure within your environment. Locking car doors, keeping a light on at night, and having someone walk you to your car are all ways of using positive control. At times a particular setting may increase your anxiety rather than make you fearful. During my years in therapy, being in large groups made me anxious. Walking into church or a meeting, I was able to ease my anxiety by scanning the room and finding someone whom I felt comfortable sitting near.

You can also control your surroundings and feel protected by using visualization. Although Rune was deceased, I remember telling my therapist I sensed his presence around me, invading my space and causing me to feel afraid. I wrote the following journal entry after a session in which I explored these fearful feelings with Dellene.

February 23, 2001

I was feeling creepy because I felt him there in the room around me. She said I should try to picture it as the energy from all of this around me, but not him. He's gone, he cannot hurt me.

By reiterating the thought *He's gone, he cannot hurt me*, I was able to control my fears in a realistic, positive way. On another occasion, I found myself feeling afraid and anxious in a grocery store, but instead of running out, I took control by visualizing blinders on my face, much like the ones racehorses wear. Because I then couldn't "see" anyone else in the store, I was able to complete my shopping.

Being your own advocate by speaking up for your needs is another positive way to take control. Later in the book, I will share an example of advocating for my needs by walking away from a movie that reminded me of my abuser. It is important to speak up and protect yourself from any situation that makes you uncomfortable.

Being an advocate also includes distancing yourself from certain people. Throughout my journey, I shared my story with friends when the time was right. Choosing whom you tell and when are good examples of maintaining a positive level of control. Most friends responded with compassion and support. There were a few people—like the couple I discussed in chapter 3, "Relationships"— whose response was to not respond. They had little or nothing to say when I told them I was in therapy for sexual abuse. When you share something so personal, silence from others is devastating. Did they not believe me? Did my story make them too uncomfortable? The only way I could have maintained their friendship would have been if I had pretended that their silence didn't bother me. Pretending was over for me—I'd done that for forty years. The difficult yet positive solution was to let go of the relationship. Healing requires being surrounded by supportive people with whom you can be yourself. By taking control and advocating for my needs, I eliminated the discomfort of being with people who were unable to support me in my journey.

Another positive outcome of advocating for my needs occurred the first Easter after I began therapy. Our tradition was to go to Clara's house for dinner—the house where my abuse took place. I hadn't shared anything with Clara about being abused or being in therapy. Although the memories were just beginning to unfold, I was anxious about returning to that house. Even so, the thought of saying we wouldn't be going there on a holiday was too much for me to bear. My children were looking forward to our traditional Easter Sunday, and Clara never would have understood if we had not gone. I wrote the following journal entry after discussing my dilemma with my therapist.

April 11, 2001

I need to make a plan A, B, and C and whatever I need to do, we do.

Plan A: I feel like I can make it through and we go—to keep things normal for the kids.

Plan B: We go and the house makes me nervous, uncomfortable. We come up with a plan to leave right after dinner. I don't know the plan yet. Either I'm not feeling well or we want to spend time with Tim's daughter.

Plan C: Either Saturday or even Sunday morning, I know I can't go—it will be too difficult to be in that house. I call and say either I'm not up to it or I'm not feeling well. In advance I will have something in the house to make for an Easter dinner for us.

I have to be sure that I make a decision based on me—not what anyone will think.

By taking control over an anxiety-provoking situation, I was able to approach the day knowing I had options. When the actual day came, we did go for dinner and left right after dessert. I did not have to contend with disappointing my children or answering questions from Clara by not attending, but when it became too uncomfortable for me to stay, we left. I was in control, and the outcome was positive.

Regulating Control

Victims of sexual abuse need to reclaim a sense of control. The question becomes one of balance within a positive range. Four strategies helped keep me within this positive range: awareness, trust, choice, and self-respect.

The first strategy is to be aware of the explicit need for control: *I am aware and accept my need to feel in control. I know my abusers stripped me of control, leaving me vulnerable and afraid. I must also be aware that my need for control can be extreme, but I can, with conscious effort, find a healthy balance.*

The second strategy is to allow yourself to trust: *I trust the people who love me and have walked this journey with me. If they make a suggestion on my behalf, it is because they genuinely care about me. I can allow them to be in control, without feeling vulnerable or afraid. Because I trust them, I listen.*

Third, when you share or relinquish control, you are still making a choice: *It remains difficult at times to accept the suggestions of those whom I trust. I can feel the need to control tugging on me even when I know their idea is right. Realizing I am making the choice, rather than letting them control me, makes the difference.*

Fourth, when your level of control is low and others are steamrolling you, respect yourself: *I respect myself enough now to say no when it isn't in my best interest to say yes. I am a survivor, whether I am sad and weak or victorious and strong. For that, I deserve respect. I am a good person who did not deserve the abuse I endured. Self-respect means knowing when to say no, keeping myself safe, and being an advocate for my needs.*

Summary

Being in control is an important factor in a survivor's life. As long as you learn to regulate it and use control in a positive way, it will not be harmful. The important things to remember are that relinquishing control is a choice and that this journey is an ongoing process. It may take time to get your need for control under control.

8
Anxiety

Anxiety is a psychological and physiological state triggered by something stressful. In some cases, it can be the result of anticipation. For survivors of sexual abuse, it is one of the many scars left in the wake of the abuse. Revealing and healing those scars will help to remediate anxiety, but until that happens, you will need a way to cope with the symptoms. In this section, I will discuss the state of anxiety that exists as a result of sexual abuse, as well as how to recognize and manage the physical and psychological symptoms.

Throughout my life, I lived with anxiety. All the symptoms were present, all the time—some days in a more dormant state, other days to a debilitating degree, and many days somewhere in between. Although my focus here is on the more extreme forms of anxiety, the following strategies can offer relief for symptoms of anxiety at any level.

I view anxiety much like living in a vacuum-packed bag. The greater the anxiety—shoulders raised, stomach tight, breathing shallow, fists clenched, teeth grinding—the more tightly packed the bag. If only we could open that bag and let in a breath of fresh air, the results would be much like letting air into a vacuum-packed bag of coffee: visualize how the grounds ease away from each other and settle into a lighter space when the seal is broken. Applying strategies to address the symptoms of anxiety renders the same result: a body physically settling down.

Physical Symptoms of Anxiety

The physical symptoms of anxiety differ for each individual, but common symptoms are:

- shortness of breath, or shallow breathing
- upset stomach
- a sense of choking
- muscle tension
- poor concentration
- susceptibility to being startled
- restlessness and difficulty sleeping

It is safe to say that you will often experience more than one symptom at the same time. Recognizing symptoms, self-talk, and self-indulgence are all means of managing these symptoms as you work toward healing.

Recognizing the physical symptoms of anxiety is a matter of being aware of your own body. Throughout my journals are statements expressing my own physical signs of anxiety:

- *I am absolutely choking tonight. I need a glass of water to wash it away.*
- *Very, very nervous, anxious, sweaty palms, tight stomach, something stuck in my throat.*
- *I've had such poor sleep. My stomach hurts—I can't focus.*
- *I have a lot of anxiety—tight muscles, telling myself to relax.*
- *I'm so anxious—tight stomach, trouble breathing, trouble eating.*

A moment of thought would make me aware that I was barely breathing or that my shoulders were raised and tight. Pain in my upper back or stomach would signal that I was tensing my muscles. My husband would point out that I was clenching my fists. When my anxiety heightened, I'd physically feel as though I couldn't swallow anything more than a sip of water.

Since anxiety impacts your physical state, ignoring these signs will lead to greater physical discomfort, whereas recognizing them will alert you that it is time to take action. You have the power to make your journey more tolerable.

Managing symptoms requires the willingness to try different options. What works for one person can create greater anxiety for another. Ask your therapist and/or your physician for suggestions. Most important, don't give up. You can find a way to take that vacuum-sealed body and let in enough air to allow the tightened fibers of your being to settle. The two strategies I found most beneficial for managing my own symptoms of anxiety were self-talk and self-indulgence.

Self-talk is one simple action that renders positive short-term results. Once I became aware of my symptoms, I'd talk to myself. If I was taking shallow breaths or having difficulty breathing, I told myself to take a few deep breaths in through my nose and out through my mouth. You can employ this technique almost anywhere—at work, in the car, in public, or alone. If you are at home, you may want to take it a step further: Lie down on your bed and close your eyes. Visualize breathing in your favorite color and breathing out black or a fiery red. Do this several times until your body relaxes.

If any part of my body tensed, again, I would talk to myself. I'd tell myself to relax my shoulders, and I would feel them drop. I'd open my fists, and my hands would settle into my lap. Once you recognize a part of your body that is tight, talk yourself into letting the tension go. To go one step further, try lying on your bed and releasing the tension in your entire body, starting with your feet and working your way up. Tell yourself to relax your toes, your ankles, your calves, and so on, until you reach your face and the top of your head. Once you get to your head, lie still, concentrating on taking slow, steady breaths. Many reputable relaxation tapes are also available to walk you through these steps; ask your therapist for recommendations.

Self-indulgence can be another effective coping strategy. Its success depends on personal preference, but the concept is universal: treat yourself to whatever brings you comfort.

A good time to treat yourself is before you go to bed. Getting a restful night's sleep when you are anxious is sometimes difficult, but concentrating on relaxing at bedtime can help. I often began by taking a hot shower, followed by drinking a cup of soothing, decaffeinated tea like chamomile or Tension Tamer. Warm milk is also a good option at night; I found it more palatable when I added a teaspoon of honey.

Although watching television can be relaxing, choose your shows carefully. Many of my favorite crime shows dealt with topics that were related to my abuse and therefore were not appropriate for viewing before I went to sleep. A better choice was to listen to soft music.

Getting a massage or a facial was also a comforting treat when I suffered from anxiety. Before you try this strategy, be aware that both a massage and a facial require allowing a stranger to touch your body, and for many victims, this act may provoke greater anxiety. But don't give up on the idea without first considering my experience.

I had headaches from the tension in my neck and shoulders. Dellene suggested that I might benefit from a massage. Having a male masseur was out of the question, and while I thought I could possibly tolerate the touch of a female, I still had reservations. Dellene's recommendation made all the difference: she suggested I tell the masseuse I was dealing with issues of sexual abuse before the massage. The thought of saying those words to a stranger added to my anxiety initially, but I was willing to try, as it would make it easier for me to ask the masseuse to stop if I was uncomfortable, and would also give the masseuse an opportunity to be sensitive to my needs. I took Dellene's advice and made the appointment.

When I arrived, the masseuse asked what music I would like and which scented lotion I preferred. It was the perfect time to speak up, but I barely got the words out: "I need for you to know I am dealing with issues of sexual abuse." Her response made it obvious that this was not the first time she had heard those words from a customer. She asked if there was any area I did not want touched and continued to ask if I was okay throughout the massage. She assured me I could tell her to stop at any point.

Throughout much of the hour, tears fell from my eyes. However, I was relaxed and in control, and the benefits were well worth it. The experience gave me the confidence to return for another massage and make the same statement prior to treating myself to a facial. This was also a good exercise in stating my needs—not something we victims are good at!

Many other ways to self-indulge can also be soothing and conducive to offering comfort for the symptoms of anxiety. Choosing your particular relaxation technique is a matter of personal preference and experience. For me, early on in therapy, Dellene suggested I go home from a difficult session and take a hot bath. The following journal entry says it all.

February 27, 2001

Oh, she said to take a hot bath. I said shower—I can't take a bath. I haven't in years. She said did you ever find that strange? Not until now. That bathroom—a place of fear. My stomach hurts. I'm going to try breathing.

My only awareness at this point was that I had a fear of the bathtub and hadn't taken a bath in many years. As relaxing as it would seem to some, it terrified me. Further along in therapy, I remembered the abusive events that took place for me in a bathtub, but initially my reaction to Dellene's suggestion, not a distinct memory, was what told me to avoid a bath.

Here, again, is an example of how important it is to be aware of and listen to your body. If I had ignored my intuition and gotten in a tub, I might have had a flood of memories or a flashback that I was not prepared to handle. Your personal experiences, as well as your reactions to strategies others present to you, are important factors to consider when choosing a relaxation technique.

Medication is an option for dealing with anxiety, as with depression, but should be discussed with a medical professional. Although I resisted medication at first, I did agree to filling a prescription for use as needed. When my anxiety was so great that I couldn't eat or sleep, I'd opt to take a low dose of my medication. Other times, my husband or therapist would recognize my level of anxiety and suggest I take medication *before* I reached such a debilitating state. It was not easy for me to listen to someone else's suggestions, but it was always best when I did, and now I know there's no reason to live in that vacuum-packed bag. Eating properly and getting restful sleep are necessary for continuing this journey. If you need medical intervention to accomplish these goals, it is important to at least explore the idea with a health care professional.

Psychological Symptoms of Anxiety

Along with physical symptoms, psychological symptoms—such as a heightened sense of fear, apprehension, and worry—are often associated with anxiety. Victims of abuse can be easily startled, triggered by certain scents or sounds; are often afraid of particular noises or silence; and can have a fear of the dark, of strange places, or of being alone. I can't recommend a way to eradicate these kinds of fears, but I can offer strategies that will help you to cope with them in a very empowering way.

First, listen to your inner voice when it tells you that you are afraid. You may be uneasy or nervous or just have a sense that something doesn't feel safe. Do not dismiss these thoughts; take control and respond in a way that will turn your fear into a safe situation. Some common examples include locking your car doors when driving, keeping your house locked when you are at home alone, and avoiding walking at night or in secluded areas. If you are leaving a large public place—such as a mall, a campus, or a movie theater—and you feel afraid, ask a security guard to walk you to your car. If a place frightens you, don't go there. If someone walking toward you makes you feel uncomfortable, cross the street. Whatever the situation, listen to your inner voice and take an active role in keeping yourself safe.

Other feelings of fear, apprehension, and/or worry will be unique to your experience with abuse. I suspect I will live with some of my own fears for my lifetime. My body still reacts to background noises, to hearing footsteps on the stairs, to dark rooms, and to being startled by someone's presence. A simple strategy for combating these feelings is to remind yourself you are no longer in an abusive setting—that is the past, and you are in the present. The smells or sounds that trigger you are just reminders of your abuse. Telling yourself that you are in the present will help to alleviate the fear.

Sometimes it will be necessary to take a more active stance to lessen your fears or apprehension. Again, doing so puts you in control. The following two examples of this approach worked well for me.

One night, I was watching a movie with a few friends. When a scene depicting an older person seductively stroking the arm of a young girl—something Rune used to do to me—began, my heart stopped beating. I became cold and sweaty. My first thought was to stay in the room, as I did not want to make my friends uncomfortable. But after a few moments of panic, I realized I had the power to protect myself. I got up and walked outside without saying a word. Within a short time, one of my friends came outside. I simply said I did not want to watch the movie; nothing more needed to be said or done. The connection to the scene in the movie brought back my fear, and my ability to take action brought me back to a safe place.

In the second example, I needed to be more explicit. A few colleagues and I were spending the weekend at a friend's home on Cape Cod. I knew the design of the bedrooms from a previous visit. One of the guest rooms had a double bed. The other two had twin beds set against the walls. As a child I slept in a twin bed, against a wall. As this girls' getaway drew closer, my anxiety grew.

At first I could not identify the cause of my fear—who would dread a weekend on the Cape with a group of girlfriends? As I thought it through, though, I realized I couldn't sleep in one of the twin beds, because my memories sickened me. I couldn't leave it to chance that I would get the room with the double bed. I tried to convince myself it was a foolish fear—no one else would understand, I was being oversensitive, I really could sleep in a twin bed—but none of my efforts to ignore the fear worked.

After discussing my reaction with Tim, I knew the only way I could go on that trip would be if I could definitely sleep in the double bed. I had to call my friend and tell her my concern. Without going into detail, I explained that I couldn't sleep in a twin bed because of my issues with abuse. I asked if she could help by ensuring that I had the bedroom with the double bed. She did not question my request; she assured me she'd take my bags and put them in the right room when I arrived. With my fears put to rest, I was able to enjoy a much-needed girls' weekend away.

Summary

The anxiety a victim experiences is related to the trauma of abuse. The way to be free from that anxiety is to do the work toward healing in therapy. The strategies I recommend are meant to relieve the symptoms associated with anxiety, not to cure the anxiety itself. There is no fear worth living with. Our situations are unique, and as survivors, we must learn to speak up and take action. Doing so is empowering, as it enables you to protect yourself from the residual symptoms caused by abuse rather than remain a victim of those symptoms.

9
Anger

The following journal entry marks my ongoing struggle with intense feelings of anger.

January 28, 2002

One year ago today, I started my first journal. When I reread it, I am amazed by all I've been through and how far I've come. Interesting, though, the one feeling that was strong then and now, that I couldn't deal with then or now—anger. For two days now I've felt it building but have no way to release it. I don't know what will work for me and I know I fight it.

In this chapter, I will discuss the anger and rage that surface as a result of sexual abuse. As I stated in the journal entry above, anger was an ongoing emotion for me, and one that I found difficult to express. Through trial and error, I learned strategies to release it, but before I could begin to implement them, I had to understand the origins of my anger and rage.

For a victim of abuse, the anger originates with the abuser but infiltrates every aspect of the victim's life. The anger is like an insect, and the abuser the core of that insect. Extending from this core are multiple tentacles crawling throughout the victim's body. Each tentacle becomes a spur of more anger and rage. Anger caused by humiliation. Anger over a childhood lost. Anger incited by a failed marriage or career or an unattainable goal. Anger related to physical and emotional pain. Anger over loss of control. Anger for the victim's belief that they deserved the abuse. Anger induced by poor self-image. Anger for living a lifetime waiting for the next shoe to drop. The list can go on, but in fact this is all anger over the destruction and pain caused by sexual abuse.

Whether a victim can relate to one or all of these examples, the anger must be addressed. Repressed anger will sit within and fester and can affect the victim's physical well-being and cause feelings of internal strangulation, as the following journal entry illustrates.

April 9, 2002

For two weeks I cried almost daily, feeling sadness. Now I think it's anger—it's bubbling up and I'm containing it. Results: back, neck, jaw ache, throat feels like it has a lump inside. I told Nancy and Tim I feel like my insides are being shrink-wrapped—sucked in tight. It's taking all of my energy.

The more you try to hold back the anger, the stronger its physical symptoms will become. Repressing anger can also cause you to turn to self-destructive behaviors. This next journal entry shares the thoughts that emerged for me as I fought to contain my anger.

June 21, 2002

It's Saturday morning. School is over. I'm spending my time containing my anger. Stomach hurts, throat tight, jaw hurts. This sucks. I can't stand to feel this way and I'm afraid to let it out. When my thoughts turn to anger, they are extreme. Crash the car, smash windows, slam myself into walls, punch, hit—it doesn't feel like it can come out any other way.

Fortunately, I did not act on any of these destructive thoughts. Despite my feeling then that at times anger "doesn't feel like it can come out any other way," it can, through the use of healthy, safe, and effective strategies.

Expressing Anger

For me, expressing anger was the opposite of what I was conditioned to do. I lived in the "perfect family," where we had no reason to express anger. I can remember only one time in my childhood when I heard my parents raise their voices. I was taught by example to respond to any disturbing situation by pretending everything was fine. In the following journal entry, I share with Dellene my confusion about and fear of this foreign feeling—expressing anger.

January 28, 2003

I got really anxious before my session. We talked about how hard it is for me to express anger. I don't know how because I never did it. Dellene's guess is I'm filled with anger, I was angry as a kid but couldn't show it. Now 1) I'm scared and 2) I don't know how to express it. I admitted that I would need to feel incredible trust and to know that she or Tim wouldn't let me get out of control. Dellene thought I could just start with thinking some angry thoughts and I also thought about writing some in this journal. So far tonight I'm not ready.

As a result of my upbringing, I had no guidelines, learned responses, or appropriate examples to follow for releasing anger. As an adult facing my past, I had to learn how to release the anger and rage that I had been suppressing for a lifetime.

Expressing anger does not come naturally for many other people, either. Whether it takes the form of verbal exertion (yelling, screaming, spewing profanities) or physical exertion (punching, pounding, or intensive exercising), expressing anger can feel awkward. Two strategies can make the process easier: letting go of inhibitions and preparing for failed attempts.

If expressing anger makes you feel uncomfortable, you can't let that be your reason to hold it in. Anger that you do not express will fester inside you and is likely to come out in a destructive way. If you are committed to healing, you must let go of your inhibitions in this respect. Experiment with different methods of expressing your anger in a healthy way, doing so in small doses, until you discover what feels right for you. If you employ these methods in the right surroundings and achieve positive results, whatever you choose will be much less embarrassing for you than exploding at the wrong person or at the wrong time.

Doing something outside of your comfort zone requires trial and error. If you decide on a trial method for expressing anger, let your inhibitions go, and give it a try, but after a few minutes you don't feel any release, chalk it up to a failed attempt. Don't be discouraged, though—know that this may happen, and be open to trying something new.

I reflect now, with a smile, on one of my own failed attempts at releasing anger. In my search for new ways to vent, my husband and I thought screaming would help. We did not want the neighbors to hear me, so we came up with a plan: We had a slide-on camper on the back of our pickup truck. Tim would drive the truck, and I would ride in the camper. We would have walkie-talkies so he could keep in touch with me. He'd drive while I screamed as loud and as long as I needed to feel some relief.

Screaming might work for some, but not for me. When I let out a small sound, it felt awkward; when I tried letting out a genuinely loud scream, it seemed forced and artificial. Instead of feeling relief, I returned home frustrated. After that and a variety of other verbal attempts, I realized my preference for releasing anger was to use forms of physical exertion, such as power walking, throwing, or pounding. Once I determined this, my methods involved activities within my comfort zone and, as a result, were more successful.

Releasing Anger

Release, according to Webster's dictionary, means *to set free; to let go or let loose; to set free from pain; a relief from emotional tension through a spontaneous, uninhibited expression of emotion.*

I perceive the release of anger as happening on three levels, like a pressure cooker. On level one, the pressure cooker is at its lowest setting, emitting just a puff of steam. On level two, as the pressure builds inside, the valve sends off a steady outpouring of steam. On level three, when the pressure has mounted to its greatest point, the valve thrusts out bursts of steam accompanied by a shrill whistle. I also associate these three levels with daily maintenance of anger, planned release, and the eruption of rage.

Level One: Daily Maintenance of Anger

Whether you experienced an entire childhood of abuse or a single incident, the anger is there. Some days, you hold it deep within your being; other days, it boils to the surface. So how do you function when you are filled with anger each day?

First, turn negative energy into positive energy. It takes an abundance of energy to repress anger; I will refer to that as negative energy, as it depletes you of the positive energy you need to function productively from day to day.

The many healthy ways to turn negative energy into positive energy include walking, running, participating in an exercise class, playing tennis or racquetball, meditation, and yoga. Any activity that results in a release of energy will work, but this is also a matter of personal preference. For example, if you dislike group workouts, then an aerobics class will not be the right choice for you, and a rigorous walk may be more beneficial.

Although these activities don't directly address anger, they will allow you to expel negative energy and enjoy the benefits—such as more positive energy, increased relaxation, and better sleep—of doing so.

Throughout my healing journey, I spent hours at the local high school track, which was located close to my home and was a safe environment if I was walking alone. The more laps I walked, the faster I went. I could almost feel the anger revving my engine. I always finished a walk exhausted but more relaxed than when I had stepped onto the track. I took this power walk at least four days a week throughout my therapy as my daily maintenance of anger.

Level Two: Planned Release

There are times when your repressed anger starts bubbling to the surface and becomes increasingly difficult to manage with a simple daily-maintenance strategy. The physical symptoms intensify. Your ability to concentrate on basic tasks falters. You're tempted to internalize the anger and fight its release. The negative energy you must use to fight the anger is draining. In addition to this generalized anger that builds, a specific incident can also incite even more intense anger. Both situations require a plan for release.

Safety is a crucial ground rule at this stage. Being safe requires that you allow someone to be with you as you plan and execute a means of releasing your anger. Once you open that valve and let some of the anger out, there's no predicting how far it will go. The possibility of turning the anger inward and hurting yourself is very real. Having someone with you serves two purposes: First, it puts you, the victim, on guard. Your awareness that someone is watching you will make you unlikely to engage in a self-destructive act. Second, if your anger does turn inward, that person can stop you from hurting yourself and help redirect your anger.

On one occasion, in a session with Dellene, what began as a healthy release of anger turned into a potentially self-destructive act. As I cried and verbalized my feelings, I also pounded the couch. At one point, I moved my fists from the couch to my thighs and continued to pound. Dellene calmly said, "Pound the couch, not your body." I moved my fists back to the couch and continued the release without hurting myself. Her gentle redirection helped me to maintain a safe release of anger.

It is imperative that you strategize with your therapist concerning the release of your own anger. Your therapist knows the most about your emotional state and can offer suggestions based on that information. In addition, whether it happens with your therapist or with a partner, it is essential that you are not alone during a planned release.

In the following journal entry, I had a plan for releasing my anger, but because I was at home alone, I was at risk of getting hurt. I wrote this entry during the period after I realized Clara's involvement in my abuse. The table I refer to is a wooden table she had given me.

February 4, 2003

It's amazing how "in control" I thought I was. After that last sentence, I felt like throwing something. Then I realized how much sense it made to smash that table from her. I went downstairs, found a broom handle. Bash! Bash! It broke—the STICK! It splintered, cut my chin, did nothing to the table. I got angrier, found another stick, finally, with stinging hands, dented the table over and over. I was so angry that I couldn't destroy it.

Fortunately, my then-seventeen-year-old daughter came home at that moment when my anger was turning to rage. Nothing would have stopped me from destroying the table, even if it meant hurting myself, but hearing her enter the house startled me and caused me to stop. I would have been horrified if she had seen me in action. Smashing the table wasn't a bad strategy; doing it alone was.

In the fall of 2004, I struggled with the decision to make a complete break from the dysfunction of my biological family, but the emotional pain was overbearing. I felt abused and abandoned by the people who were supposed to love me, and I knew it would take a great deal of work to make it through this final separation. That thought made me angry. As the anger mounted, I longed for some relief.

My friend Nancy and I met at our favorite spot for coffee and decided a power walk would help. We chose to walk right in town rather than drive to the track. After a few blocks, I stopped *thinking* about my anger and began *feeling* the intense emotion. As this transition progressed, I sensed myself shutting down. I did not want to talk; Nancy understood. My pace quickened and continued to increase with each step; she kept up. One mile passed, then two. Sunlight faded into darkness. As my anger built to rage, I turned into a racehorse with blinders—blinders that I once used to help me cope with anxiety in a crowded store. My vision narrowed, and I became unaware of my safety net, Nancy, though she was right by my side.

We came to the edge of a golf course. When I saw the open space, I began to run. My rage propelled me. I began crying, yelling, wanting to run into the darkness and never be found. Nancy caught me and pulled me to the ground. She held me as I cried until I felt as if my insides were splayed on the ground.

After some time had passed and she had assured me I was okay, we walked the two miles back to her car, arm in arm, exhausted, released from the anger and safe. Later that evening, I called my therapist to share the experience.

When Nancy and I left that coffee shop, I knew I needed to expel some of my anger, but I was unaware of its magnitude. I can't, or perhaps do not want to, imagine the outcome of that walk had I been alone. Would I have run into the street? Been stopped by a stranger? Gotten lost or hurt? I am just thankful I was with a friend and will never know what the outcome of being alone in that state of anger might have been.

Whether your anger is generalized and mounting or related to a specific incident, your strategies for planned release should be the same: choose a partner, establish parameters, and stay focused.

The most important factor to consider when choosing a partner for planned release is to select someone you trust. Remember, you may be releasing your anger in a way that feels extreme, and you will not be able to predict whether or when you will need that person to take action to keep you safe. For many, the only person you will trust to this extent is your therapist. I was blessed to have three people whom I trusted to be with me: Dellene, Tim, and Nancy.

The parameters you will need to establish for a planned release of anger are the place and the duration of your plan. The place should be one that allows for privacy without interruption, since worrying about a stranger's seeing or hearing you will inhibit your ability to release anger. Using your home for this purpose is fine, as long as you're assured no one besides you and your partner will be there during that time. Similarly, if you choose an outdoor area, you will need to be sure other people aren't present. Your therapist's office is another option, and one that will allow you complete privacy.

The duration should include enough time to prepare, release, and recover. There is no fixed length of time when you will be actively engaged in letting out anger, but the following are worthwhile considerations: Before you can expel anger, it needs time to rise to the surface, and you need time to feel comfortable enough to let it go. After a session of releasing anger, you will also need time to be in a calm, restful state.

Meanwhile, your partner will need to be attentive to the length of time you're engaged in expelling anger. If they see that you are exhausted and not stopping, it is time for them to step in and try to bring you to a quieter state. Gently placing a hand on your shoulder or asking you to take a few deep breaths may be enough settle you down.

Staying focused during this process means focusing on one source of your anger. As we discussed earlier in this chapter, many facets of abuse have the potential to incite anger, which can then build and fester and even strangle its victim. Although this anger needs to be released, it can't happen all at once. I imagine a person exploding into thousands of pieces, impossible to put back together: by choosing one object of your anger—whether a specific incident, your abuser, or a feeling—and staying focused on that, you will prevent this explosion.

Begin by saying, "I am so mad at . . ." or, "I feel so angry because . . ." or, "I hate . . ." Once you determine your focus, try to stay with it while you scream and bash. If you make your partner aware of the object of your anger, they can determine a few key phrases to help you remain focused: "How did that make you feel?" "Picture his face." "What would you want to say to her?" Involving your partner is one small strategy that could prevent a potentially big explosion.

Following are three personal examples illustrating planned release using the aforementioned guidelines. The first example demonstrates a strategy for dealing with generalized anger, the second describes a strategy I used when an occasion incited my anger, and the final example depicts a strategy I used when my anger was directed at a specific person.

In the first example, I discussed my planned release of anger with my therapist in advance and then was able to use our agreed-upon strategy several times when my generalized anger began to escalate. The complex where my friend Nancy lived had an indoor racquetball court, and, although I had never played racquetball, she suggested smacking the ball as a good outlet for anger. I was willing to give it a try. Nancy was my partner, the parameter was finding a time when the courts were not crowded, and my focus was Rune.

Rather than playing an actual game of racquetball with me, Nancy would feed me the balls and I'd smash them as hard as I could against the wall. Once I warmed up, I was less conscious of my surroundings and able to expel some sound with each hit. They began as grunts but soon after evolved into profanities or statements of anger toward Rune.

Knowing the object of my anger—in this case, Rune—and understanding my inhibition to vocalize that anger, Nancy would utter these phrases: "How do you feel about him?" "What do you want to call him?" "Say it again . . . louder!" Her encouragement helped me to focus and release more and more with each hit until I was physically exhausted. Most sessions ended with my slumping to the floor, drained and yet calm. This is a perfect example of a "trial" that ended in success. When my anger mounted, I'd call Nancy and say it was time for racquetball. It was a safe plan, I was not alone, and it relieved me of my self-destructive feelings of anger.

The following journal entry describes my need to release anger associated with an occasion: the first Christmas after I began therapy. My anger was pervasive, and I could not escape the reminder of family associated with the holiday. Dellene and I devised a plan that included a box of Christmas ornaments Clara had given me over the years. Tim would go as my partner, the parameter was a secluded area early in the morning, and my focus was my feelings toward Clara.

December 16, 2001

Last week I felt a lot of anger toward myself. At my session I was blocked at first but finally cried. On the weekend I kept busy with Christmas stuff but by Sunday morning woke up at six filled with flooding anger/pain. I had come up with a plan with Dellene to find a way to smash all the Christmas bulbs that were Clara's that I couldn't put on the tree. Sunday morning by six forty-five Tim and I were driving to find a secluded place to smash those bulbs—Timberlane golf course. I put a few at a time in a pillowcase with a can. I smashed it so hard against a tree and it felt great but it made a loud echoing noise. After a few I was too afraid that someone would hear it. We left, but it still helped.

Tim sensed my lack of focus and fear of being seen or heard. He assured me I had done a good job of getting some of the anger out, and that it was okay to let that be enough for the day. The event was planned, my husband was with me, and I accomplished my goal of experiencing relief.

I wrote the next journal entry a year into my therapy. I had been dealing with the flood of memories of being sexually abused by Rune. The entry refers to "taking him out of the box." As I explained in chapter 6, "Visualization," I used the technique of visually putting him away where he could no longer hurt me. In this case, I had visualized locking him in a coffin until I was ready to take him out. Now, my anger toward him had built to a debilitating level.

January 30, 2002

Tonight was a breakthrough. I went into my session feeling choked with anger and was able to talk about it and talk of my need for a plan. I finally faced that it's fear—fear is why I can't get it out, and also rage. So much anger can bring out rage.

It feels good to admit that it's not that I can't get my anger out, it's that I'm so scared. I decided that it was time to let him out of the box. I need him out to face him. Next visit our plan is to take him out, sit him across from me, and tell him what I think and what I'd like to do to him. Dellene said it will be hard to use the language I'll need to use but I have to. I said that I know now that I have to do this in her office (not alone) and it will take a lot of trust on my part but that I do trust her and I need to feel safe.

The plan was made: Dellene would be with me, the parameter was in her office, with my abuser out of the box, and my focus was Rune. One week later, I entered Dellene's office.

February 8, 2002

I was very nervous, didn't feel strong or confident, but knew what I had to do. It was too bright in the room—Dellene was nice enough to turn on a lamp and change the atmosphere. We put a chair directly across from me. Then we just talked a bit about my plan, my expectations, about him a little. She talked me through getting him out of the coffin and then she was silent. I put him in the chair, tied in, told him he had to look at me and couldn't talk. Then it started. I closed my eyes and clenched my fists . . .

It was forty minutes of rocking crying clenching yelling. Then it was time to put him away. I put him back in the coffin, tied and gagged. When it was over, I felt like I had come back from a different place. It was scary—I asked Dellene if I was all right. She reassured me that I was safe and okay. I was aching all over and completely drained. There are no words to describe it.

By having my therapist with me, having a plan, and staying focused on Rune, I was able to release profuse anger in a safe manner. I was left drained and slept for much of the following day. The result: instead of feeling choked with anger, I felt relieved and in a better physical and mental state to continue my journey toward healing.

The entire journey to healing is a process. If you create a plan and it doesn't work, try something else. You *will* find a safe, successful means of releasing anger eventually, as long as you are willing to try.

Level Three: Eruption of Rage

How does rage differ from anger? What sets it apart from the anger that responds to interventions such as daily maintenance activities or planned release? Rage erupts. When anger is at its peak and the pressure is unrelenting, the response is the eruption of rage. We have little or no internal control over rage. We can plan to release anger; we cannot plan to release rage. It is a brief burst of fury that can be frightening and in some instances damaging.

Although you can't plan for the eruption of rage, there are strategies that will prepare you for when it happens. Being prepared means the difference between a physically and emotionally destructive situation and one that results in a cleansing release that moves you forward in your journey.

Be aware of signs that your anger is intensifying. The physical symptoms of repressing anger become red flags. Your feelings of internal strangulation are constant. Nights of restless sleep are accumulating; your breathing is short, your stomach tight, your fists always clenched. Your thoughts sometimes turn to violent acts. You have difficulty being around people and retreat to a very isolated place within your mind. Although it seems like a logical time to increase your daily maintenance activities, your anger is consuming all your energy. You get little release from your maintenance routine and perhaps even decide to cease all physical activity. These are all indications that the release of anger may turn into an eruption of rage.

Once you are aware of your "red flags of rage," the ideal course of action is to share your symptoms with your therapist. Unfortunately, in this emotional state, it is very difficult to be insightful enough to do so. You are in what I call fighter mode: fighting the anger, fighting facing the origins of the anger, and fighting the feeling that you are losing control. Because you are using all of your energy to fight, it is unlikely that you will recognize your own need for help.

If you are fighting anger at this level, it is also possible that you'll express your symptoms to your therapist, but not the origin of the symptoms. Therapists are trained to recognize the signs and symptoms of intense anger and are therefore likely to note that the symptoms you are experiencing are related to your anger and should be addressed. In response to this suggestion, you may feel very tempted to shut down—*Don't make me deal with this! Let me keep fighting the fight!*—but the reality is, you won't be able to hide from or contain the anger for very long. Remember the ground rule about being in control and knowing when to let others be in control for you? This is a time to let others be in control for you. Listen to their concerns about your emotional state. Allow them to help you address your anger.

When you are able to open up about your feelings and listen to others, you will be ready to take the next step: being proactive. There's a difference between predicting when anger will turn to rage and *preparing* for anger to turn to rage. Rage erupts when anger is at its boiling point. There are conditions and safety nets, as I call them, that you and your therapist can decide on ahead of time to prepare for a potential eruption of rage. Discussing at a calmer time in therapy what rage might look or feel like helps make it less frightening. Discussing and accepting ahead of time that you may need to allow your partner to intervene for your safety will make it easier if it becomes necessary, because once your anger erupts in rage, you will have little control over your actions, and they might harm you. It is your partner's responsibility to stop or redirect you in order to keep you safe, as in the example I cited earlier when my therapist redirected me to pound the couch and not my body.

It is impossible to anticipate every scenario that will incite rage. Unexpected bursts of rage often happened to me when I was journaling or doing what I call "rage writing." Most times, I'd begin writing in my journal about an event, a conversation, a nightmare, a memory, etc. As my writing progressed, the focus changed from the event itself to the emotions attached to that event. The feelings intensified until it seemed the pen moved faster than my thoughts. I was a locomotive without brakes, writing fast and furious. The letters got bigger, the handwriting scrawled, the imprint from my white-knuckled grasp pressed through multiple pages. Painful, hateful words burst out of me. Sometimes these experiences ended in uncontrollable tears; other times I fought the urge to stab myself rather than the page. It was an eruption of rage without awareness, without a partner or a therapist, without a plan.

If you are experiencing these unexpected eruptions, it is important to share them with your therapist and make a strategy for the future so that you know how to handle them. Dellene encouraged me to be aware of the change in my writing, put down the pen, lie still, taking slow, deep breaths, and wait until the feelings subsided, knowing I would discuss them with her at my next appointment.

In "Level Two: Planned Release," I spoke of another time I was alone and not safe, when I tried to destroy a table and a piece of wood flew off and cut my chin. Fortunately, I was interrupted by my daughter's coming home. If she hadn't, and my anger had turned to rage, I would have been in danger of inflicting more physical harm. That table did later become the object of my rage, but because I made a plan with my therapist and my husband, the destruction occurred in a safe environment and resulted in a positive outcome.

The days leading up to this event were difficult. As I recalled Clara's participation in my abuse, I needed every ounce of my energy to repress the anger and pain I felt. I did not want to do the work of facing this part of my past. My way of avoiding it was to say I was worn out and needed a break. I fought to hold back the emotions, but, as the following journal entry illustrates, I was losing ground.

February 26, 2003

Well, the week began better but the worn-down feeling came back—tired, no energy. Dellene and I had a strange session. I dug down and cried but didn't let go, felt angry but didn't let go. Then I cried all the way home. The weekend came and Saturday I knew I had to face the anger. Tim had a talk with me. He didn't think I was "worn out." He thought I was holding back, which always drains me of energy. I agreed.

I managed to repress my anger at that therapy session, but when Tim shared his thoughts, my fight ended. My physical signs and symptoms were obvious to both my therapist and Tim. I was frightened but knew it was time to let go of control and be open to their observations. Tim suspected that when I addressed this level of anger, it would build to rage. We prepared by calling my therapist for guidance and together created a plan: I would destroy the table from Clara, making her the object of my anger. Tim would be my partner. He would find a strong implement that could do the job. He would stand in the doorway of the next room. I would call to him if I needed his help. He would intervene if he thought it was necessary for my safety. Dellene was on call during the release and for support following the event. In the following journal entry, I wrote a brief account of the episode.

February 26, 2003

I did it—it took nothing to start. I had a mason's hammer and pounded until the table started to break apart. I kept pounding, pounding, breaking off pieces until my arms couldn't take anymore. I stopped and Tim held me. He was so proud of me for how I did. I cried a little, felt more drained than ever before—emptied.

This account in my journal is mild compared with what actually occurred. I pounded that table until a pile of kindling sat in the middle of the room. My arms ached, and I could barely move. My husband stepped in and took the hammer from my hands. Rage drove that hammer—rage erupted out of me. When it was over, the absence of rage left me emptied and able to experience a few moments of peace.

Following that event, I slept on and off through the entire next day. My therapist provided positive feedback, helping me to view this tumultuous event as a great accomplishment. As frightening as it was to feel my rage being expelled from within, our plan kept me safe. In relieving myself of the gnawing pain of repressed anger, I was left with an inner peace and renewed strength to move forward. At a later therapy session, I discussed the anger that led to the incident and then processed the actual event and feelings that followed. This is an important step to take after any release of anger.

The state of calm you experience will be temporary; anger and rage will mount again. But those few moments of peace will give you hope that there is a light at the end of this dark tunnel—that at the end of your journey to healing, you will experience peace and joy. Even when you have not yet learned to anticipate that your anger is turning to rage, there is a way to be prepared and stay safe: by visualizing your inner core.

Your inner core is your center of courage and strength, the piece of you that remained whole when all other phases of your life were crumbling. Remember, you are reliving and facing abuse that happened *in the past*. You have already survived the abuse and have taken steps toward healing. The fact that you've chosen to face your demons indicates that you believe your life is worth saving, even though in moments when you are experiencing an eruption of rage, the fact that you have this strength may not come to mind. Therefore, you must prepare for those occurrences by focusing on your inner core during the less stressful phases of your therapy. By doing so, you will find that your core strength is instinctively there to keep you safe during the toughest challenges.

I wrote the following journal entry after a conversation with my therapist, in response to my fear that I was losing ground. I had shut down and was unable to feel any emotion.

September 19, 2001

She assured me I'm going to be okay. I told her I was scared because there was a core of me—all my own—that survived all of this and after last night I feared I was losing that core, that piece of myself that remained untouched by him. I haven't lost it even if temporarily it feels like I did. He can't kill that part of me. It is the piece that made me a good wife, mother, teacher, friend. It is my soul.

My abusers did not ruin me then, and I would not allow them to ruin me now. I needed constant reminders that my core would give me strength when I needed it most. When I was alone and unsuspecting that my anger was turning to rage, there came a point when I'd tell myself to stop: stop writing, stop yelling, do not give in to the urge to inflict pain. I would call out to my husband, call my therapist, or lie still until I was in a safer place. The scene could have spiraled into something I'd later regret. The reason it didn't, the reason I was able to bring myself to safety, was that my inner core took hold. The following journal entry is one example of my inner core protecting me from self-harm.

May 23, 2002

I was so anxious and angry tonight. Nancy and I took a fast power walk. I did some talking and swearing. Mostly right now, today, I'm afraid that I'm fighting something. Pushing something back. I don't want another fucking memory! I hate this! STOP— JUST STOP STOP STOP! I can't write any longer. I need to distract myself, read, get away from this.

In this journal entry, my anger escalated. Taking a power walk gave me little relief, as my anger stemmed from my not wanting to face another memory of abuse. As I wrote that I wanted the memories to stop, I realized the writing had to stop, too. I was raging and feared where that rage would take me. My inner core gave me the strength to put my journal aside and distract myself until I was able to address the rage in a safe setting. In this instance, I dropped my pen and journal on the floor and lay still on my bed. Tim came upstairs to check on me. Seeing the state I was in, he encouraged me to get up, take a hot shower, and change my thoughts by watching television with him. If I had been alone, I would have called my therapist for support.

There will be times in this journey when your only means of survival will be to rely on your inner core. Realize that you are a survivor, and gain strength from knowing that your abuser(s) did not ruin you then and you will not let them ruin you now! The following journal entry is an affirmation of my inner core that continues to bring me strength today.

September 19, 2001

So here is the piece I must remember through all of this. My whole life I felt different from my family. There was a small piece of me that was all my own. It survived through all of the terror, pain, fear, and loneliness. It gave me strength to live. It allowed me to love and be loved. If that core survived then, it will survive now. He took everything from me but that core. He cannot take it or destroy it now. He's dead. I am alive.

Yes, you can be prepared even when you are alone, unsuspecting of the rage and without a plan. That inner core that gave you the strength to survive the abuse will now give you strength as you face the hardest moments in your journey to healing.

Summary

Releasing anger is not a onetime event. Your anger will subside with each occurrence and then build again as you recognize and address new phases of your abuse. However, it is important to remember that with each release, you are moving a step closer to being cleansed and whole. Getting the anger out allows room for peaceful, joyful feelings to seep in.

For me, expressing anger became easier with time. My initial fears subsided once I realized I was not going to fall apart or lose control. After some time, I began to recognize the benefits of letting anger go. Although I was never eager to address my anger, I gained confidence in knowing I could do it safely and would feel better once I did.

The most exciting revelation for me is that, while my memories of abuse still sadden me and even frighten me at times, the debilitating anger that once infiltrated my whole being is gone and will not return. I am free!

To release means to set free. Once you release your anger, you will set yourself free—free to feel joy, free to see light versus darkness, free to believe you are on the road to living the life you so deserve.

10
Depression

We've all experienced feeling "down in the dumps" or disappointed, and many people describe that state as depression, as in "I'm so depressed that my team lost last night."

But when your symptoms of depression last for more than two weeks and interfere with daily living, you may be considered clinically depressed. This is the depression I will speak of in relation to survivors of sexual abuse, and the condition I will attempt to help you better understand by sharing examples and strategies based on my personal experience and readings.

If you are experiencing symptoms of depression, it is important to speak with your therapist or health care provider. Medication is a viable and often necessary option used to manage depression, as long as it is taken under a doctor's care. Throughout much of my journey, I resisted antidepressants, telling myself, *I can handle this; I don't want to feel like a zombie; I don't want medication to impede the progress I'm making; I will not give up control.* But allowing myself to exist in a depressed state without medical intervention *was* giving up control. I could barely function.

With my husband's support and my therapist's assurance that I was not losing control, I made the decision to seek medical advice and ultimately chose to take medication. At a time when you feel your life is slipping away, it is crucial to feel as if you're maintaining some control. It is an individual choice, but if you are depressed, I strongly suggest that you speak to a medical professional and make an informed decision regarding medication. In the following journal entry, I finally admitted that I was depressed.

August 7, 2003

So where am I right now, honestly? Depressed. I sleep most of the day away. Unmotivated—can't even think of what to do, let alone do it. Angry. We can't take any more. Fighting—trying to hold on, stay in the present, keep faith.

What else? I nervous-eat and then hate my weight and body—no exercise, very critical of self.

There are many levels and symptoms of depression that survivors experience throughout their journey to healing. These factors differ from person to person, but they all affect daily living. The good news is that once your scars of abuse have healed, your depression will give way to joy. But in the meantime, it can be debilitating when those who suffer from depression do not understand its symptoms and have no strategies for coping with it. This chapter offers many such examples and strategies.

The symptoms of depression fall into three categories: changes in thinking, changes in motivation, and changes in behavior. Chronic sadness can also be a symptom of depression and, as you will see, may resurface long after your healing journey is complete.

As a victim works through the stages of healing and becomes whole, anger, pain and anxiety are replaced by contentment and joy. However, as wonderful as life is, there are still times when sadness returns, whether it is caused by a special event, such as a birthday or a holiday; a memory of the past; or hearing an account of someone else being abused.

At the end of my teaching career, I was honored at a retirement party. Several people spoke on my behalf; my friends, husband, and children were all there to enjoy the evening with me. Days later, I found myself wallowing in sadness and couldn't understand why. It had been less than a week since I had experienced one of the most special nights of my life. After sharing my thoughts with Tim, I realized that my sadness stemmed from my biological family's absence at the party. Then it made perfect sense: I needed to recognize the feeling and express it by allowing myself to cry. Once I did that, I felt relieved and able to move forward.

What's important to note is that once you're healed, even if your sadness does return, it will remain for only a brief time. It is normal and quite different from being depressed. Sometimes simply expressing the feeling or having a good cry are enough to release the emotion and return you to a more serene place.

Changes in Thinking

Depression can also cause changes in thinking, characterized as loss of concentration, negative thoughts, and poor self-esteem. Loss of concentration affects simple, routine tasks, such as paying bills on time or remembering an appointment. Diminished concentration affects more important aspects of life, such as job-related responsibilities. The more details you forget, the more delinquent you are, the worse you will feel, and that will only add to your depression. Fortunately, a simple strategy—making lists—can prevent an embarrassing outcome.

To complete routine tasks, get into the habit of creating daily lists. Most mornings before work, I made a list of what I needed to achieve that day, such as calling for a dentist appointment or sending a birthday card. It is important to be realistic and write things you know you can accomplish—a list of ten errands when you are already overwhelmed will only add to your depression.

When it came to my job, I learned the importance of creating a list for the following day before I left work. Not knowing what my night would bring—little sleep, a nightmare, etc.—I could not risk arriving at work and not being able to focus on where I had left off and what I needed to address. My list allowed me the best possible start even after the worst possible night.

Negative thoughts, the second change in thinking that comes about during a depression, can be described as looking at the dark side of everything or seeing the glass as half empty. For me, that murky swamp of negative thoughts included living in a world of what-ifs: *What if I say or do the wrong thing? What if something terrible happens to Tim? What if . . .* always ending in a negative. I expended energy creating negative hypothetical situations that were unlikely to occur.

Other negative thoughts related directly to my abuse. As a child, I never knew when the next incident would occur. Would he come to my room that night? I realize now that I lived my life waiting for the other shoe to drop. Time would pass and life would go on, but there would always be a next time.

Waiting for something bad to happen became a way of life after my abuse as well. If things at work, at home, or in any phase of my life were going well, I'd think about what was going to happen next. When would the turn of events take place? When was something going to go wrong? When would the darkness return?

It isn't easy to stop these negative thoughts when they've become the norm, and it's therefore very difficult to even be aware that you're dwelling in the negative. However, the work you're doing to heal needs to include a conscious assessment of your emotional well-being. Ask yourself, *Where am I hovering?* If the answer is *In the negative*, it is time to try stopping those thoughts.

This might not be possible during the most challenging stages of your journey, but managing your emotions some of the time, or at least being conscious of them, is better than nothing at all. So when you recognize your thoughts swerving to the dark side, my suggestion is first to stop the thoughts, then to make a conscious effort to change them. Intentionally think of something positive, or try to remember a time or an event in your life when you were happy or at peace. Force yourself to revisit the sights, the sounds, and the smells of those positive events. If that doesn't work, turn on the radio, lose yourself in a television show, create any distraction. Whatever the technique, it will help pause the negative and create a more positive train of thought.

Poor self-esteem is the third change in thinking that occurs during a depression. Poor self-esteem, victim of abuse—the two go hand in hand. The act of the abuse leaves the victim feeling damaged and worthless. In some cases, victims believe they are deserving of the abuse. For a child who has been abused, there's no way to make sense of this terrible thing that's happening, so the child rationalizes it by thinking they're "bad" or that they must deserve to be treated this way. I can surmise that an adult victim feels like an object—used, hurt, and tossed aside. There's nothing about the act of sexual abuse toward a child or an adult that can foster good self-esteem, and with low self-esteem comes self-criticism. Your mind constantly evaluates your own looks, words, and actions, and the grade is always the same: failing.

I never measured up because I was the one who was chosen to be abused, so there must have been something wrong with me. I can still hear Clara and Rune telling me I was "the big one," I was "the clumsy one," I was "too emotional." In the following journal entry, I begin to explore the thought that I was not at fault.

August 3, 2001

I spent forty years of my life consciously or unconsciously believing there was something wrong with me. He chose me to hurt. My mother chose not to protect me. I wasn't worth it. So now I have to work at changing those thoughts. I am the victim. He is the hated one, not me.

How do you change your self-image? How do you erase the tapes that have been playing in your head for years?

First, believe you did not deserve the abuse. Believe there is no value in the words or actions of your abuser. Believe others love you, and with time begin to love yourself. For me—and, I would guess, most victims—this is a long, ongoing process. One strategy is to think of someone who tells you they love you. Do you respect that person? Do you trust their judgment about other things? If you do, then realize you should also trust their judgment about you. Believe they love you for good reason, and your self-image will begin to change.

Years into my healing journey, I have continued to work on

believing that the people who tell me they love me do in fact love me. It is as much about trust as it is about believing I am lovable. I innately trusted my parents, yet they were the ones who hurt me, so how could I trust that others really cared? I wrote the following journal entry after I shared my feelings about love with Tim.

March 6, 2001

When he said, "You are the woman that I love so much and your father molested you—don't you think that's affecting me? I love you . . ." Well, that opened another door for me and a flood of tears. I admitted to Tim that I don't believe that I'm loved that much, don't feel worthy. Your parents are supposed to love you more than anyone. He did it to me and she didn't do anything about it. I wasn't worth the trouble it would cause. How could I think that someone loves me as much as Tim loves me?

Six years and seven months later, I continued to struggle with believing I deserved to be loved, as the following journal entry illustrates.

October 23, 2007

I am in a new phase. Some things feel very different. I've been cruising along but it is time to work. What are the issues? 1) Very big: accepting myself, believing I am lovable, understanding what it means to be loved, loving Tim fully as he so deserves, trusting!

The strategies I have suggested may seem overly simplistic to address such difficult issues, but sometimes it takes little steps to make big gains. And if you're going to cope with the changes in thinking that accompany depression, even the slightest modification can be uplifting.

Changes in Motivation

Depression can decrease motivation and interest in many pursuits, whether it is a new activity, a daily task, or a favorite hobby. Almost everything becomes a chore. Some days it is difficult to even get out of bed. In my experience, Monday through Friday, going to work became the catalyst for me to move, whether I had the energy or not. The thought of calling in sick was more unsettling than getting ready to go out the door. How do you move from that bed or chair when the weight of depression is holding you down?

One strategy to improve motivation is to find an incentive. Think about one small pleasure or reward you would like to give yourself. When my alarm went off on mornings when I was depressed, I'd lie in bed for a few minutes and think about one incentive that might help me get up. Some days it was as simple as realizing I had a new outfit to wear or that I could buy a Dunkin' Donuts coffee on the way to work. Other days it would be the realization that in eight hours I could crawl back into bed without feeling guilty about missing a day of work. Whatever your personal incentive is, give it a try.

Because depression can make the simplest activity feel overwhelming, facing an entire day may feel insurmountable, so a second strategy for addressing a change in motivation is to view the day in small increments. My daily increments started as small as this: *Just get up and into the shower, and then decide if you can make it to work.* Once I made it through a shower, I tackled getting dressed. When I was ready to go out the door, my next step was to conquer the drive. Sometimes these small steps were my only means of moving through a day.

Depression can also create a yearning to stay still, void of any activity or even of thoughts. Even the simplest task, such as a trip to the grocery store, can elicit symptoms of depression. On weekends and days off, I can remember sitting on the couch, trying to motivate myself to do something, anything. I'd think of something I used to enjoy, like cooking: *Maybe I can get up and make a pot of soup.* But then the thought of the steps it would require—getting out ingredients, preparing, cleaning up—would make me feel physically ill. I couldn't possibly manage everything.

My first response would be to give in to the pit in my stomach and dismiss the idea. My body felt like dead weight. It was much easier to stay still. Reading wouldn't work; I would scan the words and lose attention. It is important to note here that a day of doing nothing is okay, perhaps even necessary, to renew your energy. It is when days go by, weekends pass, and you haven't accomplished a thing that you should consider taking charge and push to address the effect of being immobilized from depression.

The next strategy to improve motivation is to get tough—pull up your bootstraps and take action. I would literally tell myself to get up and do something: throw in a load of wash, make a bed, prepare a meal, any activity requiring me to move. Once up, I often had enough motivation to accomplish one more task. It also helps to set a time frame for when you will begin an activity and when you will end—*At two o'clock, I will get up and begin a task. At four, I'll allow myself to take a rest*—as well as to do things in small stages: *First, I'll make a cup of tea. If I get that far, I may find a recipe to tackle.* With each success, you will find it becomes easier to stay active.

The next strategy for addressing a change in motivation involves another person, someone you can put on guard. Tell that person that you are unmotivated and are spending days immobilized. Ask for their help. It is much easier to say no to yourself than to say no to a loved one or a friend.

After a while, it wasn't necessary for me to say anything to my husband. He would know when it was time to push. Asking me to accompany him to Home Depot would get me up and out, and would often lead to my having the motivation to take on my own task.

If your lack of motivation is upsetting, and staying in bed is causing you to feel guilty and not rested, it is probably time to give in to someone else's suggestion. Going for a walk, out to lunch, or for a drive can get you out of your "funk" for some period of time. This is a perfect example of the ground rules that distinguish between being in control and knowing when to let others be in control for you. If you put someone on guard and make them aware of your mood, they will be more likely to step in and get you moving. The following journal entry illustrates the positive results of having someone "on guard."

February 23, 2003

Friday we left for Boston for two nights. It was the best thing we could have done. I had told Dellene how much I needed a break from this bedroom. I spend so much time alone in here. The weekend was worth a hundred therapy sessions. Relaxing, fun, intimate, pampering. Tonight I feel so much better. What will the week bring? I don't know but I do know I feel better tonight and I'll hold on to that. Thank you, God.

It was my husband's idea that we get away for the weekend. He knew I needed a change. This time, I was able to give up some control and trust his judgment. Although I wasn't enthused initially, as I later wrote in my journal, I benefited from knowing we were not spending another weekend confined to our home.

This final strategy for addressing motivation is necessary when someone else's idea doesn't work, when what begins as a good plan of action becomes overwhelming. This is a time to listen to your body and express what you need. You shouldn't go along with a plan designed to help you if it is more than you can handle. As much as you may want to, it isn't wise to follow through on plans to please someone else.

I remember a night when my husband thought it would be good for me to get out and have dinner with friends. This couple knew my situation. We hadn't been out on a weekend in weeks, maybe even months. Part of me thought it could be enjoyable; part of me felt guilty that Tim had sacrificed every weekend to stay home with me. He deserved a night out.

As we were driving to our friends' house, I wouldn't talk. I stared out the window, pulling deeper into myself with each mile. When Tim asked, "Where are you?" I started to cry and responded I couldn't go through with it; I couldn't be with people this night. He pulled over, called our friends, and canceled our plans. Once he assured me it was okay, we were able to stop and have a quiet dinner alone. By acknowledging and expressing my feelings and modifying the plan, we were able to salvage the night and enjoy our time together.

Changes in Behavior

Behavioral changes—namely, social withdrawal, change in appetite, and apathy—are another major development that occurs during a depression. When we look back on the effects of depression we've discussed so far—loss of concentration, negative thoughts, poor self-esteem and self-criticism, lack of motivation, loss of interest—is it any wonder social withdrawal becomes another manifestation of depression? Any type of social event requires at the very least making a plan, getting ready, and engaging in conversation. Activities you might once have looked forward to become dreaded events in the face of depression. The seemingly simple solution is to stay home—but is it that simple?

Because this journey to healing is a long process, it isn't healthy to isolate yourself during this entire time. In fact, a comfortable level of social interaction can represent a necessary distraction and a respite from all the hard work you're doing. In addition, some events are almost impossible to avoid—a relative's wedding, for example—and creating and explaining an excuse for not attending can be more stressful than the event itself.

What strategies can you use to balance the urge to pull the covers over your head with the need to engage in some social interactions? First, avoid impulsive responses to invitations so that you can make well-thought-out decisions. Quite often people get caught off guard by a verbal invitation and respond immediately. Instead, be prepared with the response "I'll get back to you." This will allow you time both to decide whether the event you have been invited to is one that you can handle and to put parameters on your involvement. You may feel you couldn't handle sitting through dinner with friends but would enjoy stopping by for a cocktail or dessert.

It also helps to think about who will be involved in the gathering. Is it a large group, one couple, people who know your plight, or casual acquaintances? The right setting depends on you and how you're feeling at the time. There were times in my journey when I preferred a large group because I could choose not to talk and get lost in the crowd. Being with one couple would put too much pressure on me to converse and be engaged. At other stages of my journey, a large crowd seemed overwhelming and I could handle only the intimacy of a quieter evening with one other couple.

A final thought: it always helps to attend events with another person, someone with whom you feel comfortable and safe. I seldom went anywhere without either Tim or my friend Nancy. They were my strength if I needed it, my safety net if I felt uncomfortable, and sometimes my excuse to leave an event early.

Another important strategy for coping with social situations is knowing when to say no. There will be some events that would be far too difficult for you to attend. You may be asked to go to a movie containing subject matter related to some aspect of your abuse. You do not need to be there. There could be people attending an event who make you uneasy or remind you of your abuser. Protect yourself from that situation. The day or date of an event may not be conducive to your making plans; perhaps it is after a therapy appointment or on a date that triggers an upsetting memory. Avoid putting yourself in that place.

At times it will be easy to just say you can't make it, but this is not always so. If you're feeling pressured to attend, you should prepare yourself with a stronger response. "I know you want me there, but please respect that I can't make it this time." "I'd be there if I could, but it just isn't possible right now." If you follow my first suggestion of not responding right away, you'll have time to develop a response that sends a clear message and that you are comfortable with.

The most difficult situation for me occurred when my uncle passed away. His daughter, my cousin and close friend, knew my story. He was married to my father's sister, Grethe, who, at the time, knew nothing of my abuse. Attending the wake and funeral would mean seeing my father's two brothers, men who physically resembled the wretched man who abused me. It would also mean seeing Clara, my mother, Rune's partner in the abuse. How could I ever be in the presence of these people, yet how could I explain my absence to my aunt? After talking it through with Tim, I knew I could not subject myself to the level of emotional trauma that would result from seeing these people. The following journal entry describes my anguish over facing this situation.

April 21, 2002

Today I got a call that Uncle Sam died. While on the phone I got the info and felt the hardest part would be running into Clara. I would have to find out when she was going to the wake. When I got off the phone I went into a panic. How could I see his sister and two brothers? Similar looks, mannerisms—I would freak. I couldn't take it. I began to feel so scared, I can't even describe my fear, terror—I'm still feeling it hours later. I called Tim upstairs to talk to me. He calmed me down and made me realize I didn't have to go to the wake. The only person that mattered was my cousin and she would understand, and if she didn't I still couldn't do it.

Soon after my talk with Tim, I called my cousin. She respected my feelings. We agreed I should be the one to tell my aunt I would not be attending the services. I planned my conversation and made the call, which I describe in the following journal entry.

April 23, 2002

I was so nervous but I knew what to say. "I'm so sorry about Sam. I have to tell you there are circumstances I can't change and I won't be able to be there." She said that's okay but I just hope you're all right. I said I am and I won't bother you with the details but please know that I would be there if I could.

As a result, I felt relieved not to be in that fear-filled environment, saddened that I couldn't be there for my aunt and cousin, and thankful that my response was accepted without question. This example illustrates the importance of knowing when to say no.

My final strategy for social withdrawal caused by depression is quite different from the first two. It addresses the rare occasion when you are up for having a good time. When you are entrenched in sadness, pain, and anger, it is still possible to have moments when you can put your issues aside and have fun.

I can remember telling my therapist that I felt guilty about having enjoyed a particular social event. Her words still ring in my ears: "It's okay to have fun, you know."

But I *didn't* know. I felt guilty and needed to be told. The hard work, pain, and progress of therapy aren't going to disappear because you've permitted yourself to leave it behind for an evening. If you feel up to a night out, go. If you want to laugh and have fun, do it! You deserve a break from the work of a survivor, and it will surely boost your strength for the continuing journey.

A second behavioral change induced by depression is a change in appetite. Whether you're eating your way through depression or not eating at all, you are compromising your health. Many people use food as a comfort, a way to fill the emptiness that accompanies depression. Although they might have a few moments of pleasure while eating, food cannot eradicate emotional pain. As the emotions resurface, the eating cycle continues. Instead of helping people to feel better, overeating often results in unwanted weight gain and loss of energy.

The opposite of overeating as a means of coping with depression is to refrain from eating. I found that when I was depressed, my desire to eat diminished and the thought of food became repulsive. When my body told me I was hungry, I'd try to think of what might appeal to me, but each idea of food made me queasy. Nothing appealed to me, not even my favorite dishes. Some days my anxiety was so strong, I imagined I was choking and believed food couldn't possibly go down. A few crackers, a cup of tea, or a small yogurt would become my meal. The results of not eating— primarily, weight loss and lack of energy—are as damaging as those of overeating.

Whether you're becoming too heavy or too thin, others will notice a change in you. They may raise questions you're not ready to answer: "Are you okay?" "Have you been sick?" People are more apt to ask questions if you've lost weight; however, if you've gained weight, it is easy to surmise when others are wondering why. Having to leave the house in clothes that are either too loose or too tight only adds to the already-difficult task of walking out the door, and looking drawn or too heavy adds to poor self-image. Most important, poor eating often results in poor health.

How can you control your eating habits and stay healthy while dealing with depression? For overeaters, portion control helps prevent weight gain; most diets recommend eating smaller portions four times per day to maintain proper weight. And for those who have no desire to eat, when the thought of eating half a sandwich is more manageable than the prospect of facing a complete meal, making healthy choices for those smaller meals is equally important. Eating four candy bars per day is *not* the idea behind small portions.

A second strategy for dealing with changes in appetite due to depression is to make a commitment. If you have committed to doing the work of a survivor—therapy sessions, facing your demons, taking the journey out of the darkness—then a part of that commitment must be staying physically healthy. Think of it as part of your fight to survive. If you're not healthy, you will not have the strength you need to do the work. Under normal circumstances, people have difficulty completing daily tasks when their resistance or energy is low or they're fighting an illness. For the survivor at work, poor health can make every part of the journey more difficult. By making a commitment to eating small portions more frequently, it is possible to stay healthy during this difficult time.

The final change in depression-related behavior is apathy. The definition of *apathy* ranges from indifference to feeling little or no emotion. Without minimizing indifference, I'll focus here on the more extreme end of the apathy spectrum: a complete lack of emotion.

Feeling nothing—a state of numbness, as I often called it when I was experiencing it—is one of the most devastating states a victim of abuse and depression can fall into. This happens at times when one's emotions are so raw, when the pain or anger is so intense, that the mind's defense is to become numb. It is both a buffer against gnawing pain and a frightening sense of nonexistence. You can maneuver through days in this state, but eventually it becomes a very uncomfortable place to hide. Humans are meant to feel. The joy of living is to feel life, both the positive, such as love, happiness, and excitement, and the negative, such as sadness, anger, and pain. For me, feeling nothing not only was unnatural but was frightening.

The following journal entries, spanning several years, are three of many that express my state of numbness or nonexistence, which was in fact always connected with an abundance of emotional pain.

October 24, 2001

I'm numb to feelings tonight. It's like I'm on novocaine. That's okay—I need it. Last night was too much for me to relive today. Tomorrow I'll go back to work.

November 20, 2002

She wouldn't come, she didn't care, she said I made too big a deal of it. She wasn't nice—she was ugly cold hard mean, she wouldn't comfort soothe hold nurture protect love support—so why do I want her? Oh, the control I have—still I can't let this go! You baby! Yes, I was a baby left to survive on my own. It hurt. I was scared. Oh, the control.

The words. I have all the words and no feelings—insulated, numb.

January 17, 2005

At 7:20 AM the house is quiet. No—Tim just called down to check on me. I need some time alone. To feel, to just let it flow, no control. No stopping, no analyzing. Something feels awful. I'm sitting in my living room but I feel detached. I could easily not be here. I need to allow myself to feel this. Invisible, unattached, unknown. If this were the last day of my life, would it matter? What's happening to me? I can't feel any emotional attachment. I can only sit, breathe, stare, and occasionally write a sentence. Hollow. I want to feel but I have no feelings.

As frightening as the emptiness I felt was, it was my body's defense against emotional anguish. It was also the place I retreated to as a young girl, as a mechanism to survive my abuse. Emotionally insulating myself became an automatic response to pain.

It may help to understand this state of being by creating a visual. Your body is a container bursting with emotional pain. If you let in the slightest bit of feeling, you will pop, much like a huge balloon. Picture the balloon popping, the escaping air forcing the balloon to fly in every direction. You have no control over the direction in which it is going. To prevent this from happening, you tightly wrap your entire body in plastic. Nothing can get in, and nothing can seep out. You are insulated, protected, well defended. You are now in a state of "numbness."

While you make the journey toward healing, you are very likely to experience this emotionally guarded state. How do you cope with the feelings that come up without becoming numb to them? How do you move from numbness to letting some feelings in? There is no easy answer to this question, but there are two strategies that can help. You can employ the first at home, but you should utilize the second only in your therapist's presence.

In a state of numbness, you can feel protected and frightened at the same time. If you're at home, it is best to try techniques that will have a calming effect, not techniques that will precipitate a release. Think of these activities as nurturing your mind. A hot cup of tea was my comfort beverage, and, although relaxation tapes are an option, I preferred soft music. I can anticipate every note of my Jim Brickman CDs from the countless times I listened to them as a means of comfort. Two of my friends gave me a prayer shawl. It was pale yellow, soft, and warm. At times, the sensory input of wrapping myself in that shawl or in an afghan, or holding a soft pillow, also soothed me. Most times when I was in my protection mode, being in Tim's arms was too risky, as his gentle touch might break my barrier and cause the emotions to pour out. At those times I'd find comfort in lying next to him, knowing I was safe, being cared for but still in control.

As I nurtured my body, I found I'd relax just enough to get through the hour, or perhaps fall asleep for a bit of needed rest. It was not enough to melt through the insulation, but just enough to put me in a more serene state. These nurturing moments also eased my fear that I was emotionally detached.

Once you are in the presence of your therapist, it is safe to move on to the next strategy. Remember that you are tightly wrapped, not letting anything in or out. It is now okay to create a small tear in that wrapping. The idea is to let a bit of feeling seep in or ooze out. It is best to do this slowly, rather than letting all of the pain escape at once. If that balloon pops, it will be very difficult to put the pieces back together. Also, what works one time may not work the next and often depends on how well defended you are at any given moment. When I was willing to allow a fragment of my emotions to ease out, one of the following scenarios was most often what created a small tear in my own balloon.

My therapist's office had become a safe haven, a place where I realized the deepest and darkest parts of my story. Sometimes merely walking into that space was enough to penetrate my guard. I would walk in, sit in my usual spot, and begin to cry. No words were needed—just a release of tears.

Other times when I entered Dellene's office, my defenses were still strong. I hated the numbness but was not willing to feel. Often she would ask, "What's going on?" The question, Dellene's soft voice, the safe surroundings, and our trust were enough to cause my tears to well up, and in a short time I was able to cry.

On other occasions, I had myself in maximum security. I was not willing to expose *any* of my emotions, yet it was evident that I could no longer go on in this state of numbness. I presented as either distant or angry, making little or no eye contact, detached. Dellene would probe a bit, asking questions that might get through my barrier and create the tear I sought. She would suggest that I take a few deep breaths, breathe into my feelings, close my eyes, and try to relax. Sometimes initiating conversation that would naturally elicit some reaction helped start the process. "How are your children doing?" "What's going on at home?" "You look tired. Have you been sleeping?" As hard as I tried to fight letting any feelings in, somewhere in my mind I knew I couldn't go on feeling numb. It took more work for both of us, Dellene and me, but at some point I would respond, open up, and let out some of the tears.

With each situation, once I began to release the emotions, I needed to hear the comforting words my therapist offered: *let it go, you are safe, you're not alone.* It is important to note that the goal of these sessions was to experience the feelings and not deal with the underlying issues, so very few words were expressed.

The degree of release afterward varied. Some nights I left completely drained, exhausted from crying for an entire session. Other nights I was willing to let only the slightest bit of feeling emerge and left the office "rewrapped" until the next session. In either case, the outcome had value, as I left knowing two things: 1) letting out a single teardrop or a flood of tears was evidence that I was still alive, I had feelings, I was not completely numb; 2) I knew I was safe. I did not crumble into a thousand pieces from this small release. Maybe next time I could do more.

It is frightening and nearly impossible to stay emotionally insulated for long periods of time. Nurturing yourself and letting out some of these emotions can bring relief.

Summary

Depression can create changes in thinking, motivation, and behavior that can be debilitating. In its mildest stage, depression interferes with your ability to cope with everyday life. In its darkest stage, it can rob you of life itself. I hope the strategies I have offered in this chapter will inspire ideas about how to cope with depression, but it is important as well to discuss your symptoms with a professional and to consider taking medication. It is nearly impossible to avoid changes in thinking, feeling, and behavior associated with depression, but it is very possible to live with the changes by easing the disruption and distress they cause.

Depression is blinding. You are living in darkness, unable to see a light at the end of the tunnel. When I was depressed, I never thought I'd feel any other way. As a survivor who has walked this journey, I want to send this message loud and clear: it is possible to feel, love, enjoy, be motivated, be happy, and just live! Depression does not have to be your existence for a lifetime. The way out of that dark tunnel is long and hard, but it leads to a life in which you will not only survive but thrive!

11
Through the Darkness

If I am going to say it out loud, I must say it all.

There's a dark side to this journey that is difficult to discuss, though without it the book would still appear complete. However, I would be denying the reader one of the most important strategies necessary for healing. The fact is, darkness happens. I gain the courage to expose the darkest days of my journey from the belief that my openness will lend courage to others, so that they, too, can make it through their darkest moments.

As you read this chapter, dwell not on the sadness but on the profound, positive thought that I walked through the darkness and I am on the other side, healed and whole. I made it! However, I am ready to revisit the darkness head-on now, in order to share with you the strategies that allowed me to fight the battle and emerge victorious.

First, what is the darkness? It is a result of intense emotional pain. Two of the gravest responses to emotional pain are self-injury and suicide, both of which I will discuss here in some of my most candid journal entries; I will also offer personal reflections on my gravest moments and the tactics that helped me make it through.

January 24, 2003

I could picture over and over last night being in front of a huge audience, saying, "Can I tell you how much pain I am in?"

There were times throughout this journey when I wanted to shout from a mountaintop, "I am emotionally crippled with pain!" The desire to tell arose in part because my cries as a child went unanswered when I desperately needed someone to hear me. My learned response in childhood was to hide my pain, push it aside, and pretend I was okay. The two most important adults in my life got up each day pretending nothing had happened. We learn from our parents, and I learned well to pretend. But the emotional pain remained buried within me. When I was an adult facing my past and reliving my memories of abuse, my need to be heard surged, and I could finally express and acknowledge my emotional pain.

As you will see in the dates of the following journal entries, the intensity of emotion does not reach a onetime high and then go away. A new memory or aspect of the abuse can cause pain to resurface and intensify. Throughout the six years of my healing journey, debilitating pain reared itself many times, and with each dark passage I was certain it had to be the last. What more could I remember? What more could be buried in the chambers of my heart? Yet it is impossible to predict what more is to come. What *is* possible is to build an arsenal of strategies that you can draw on each time your emotional pain builds, and that will become weapons in your fight against the urge to respond to pain with self-injury or suicide.

Self-Injury

The term *self-injury* generally refers to inflicting physical pain as a coping mechanism to relieve emotional pain. It is more prevalent among young adults, with a higher incidence in young women. The self-injury I will discuss in this chapter refers specifically to the urge to inflict pain and the fight against that urge. The difference is, those who are self-injurers repeatedly act on the urge. Some victims of sexual abuse fall into this category and require professional interventions, which I am not qualified to discuss. The strategies I will share are for others like me, who experience the urge without causing injury.

Why would anyone want to self-inflict pain? Looking back on my journey, I can identify three answers to that question. First, self-injury is a means to communicate a need for help without using words: *Maybe someone will see that scratch or cut, and maybe they will ask where it came from, and then maybe they will know how much I am hurting and they will help me.*

What a sad way to reach out—yet in times of despair, it is sometimes impossible to put words to the pain and ask for help. There were many times when I wasn't ready to verbalize my pain. I could talk all around it without expressing what I really felt. "I can't stop moving. I have to be doing something all the time." "I wake up as tired as when I went to bed." "I feel so tight." "I feel nothing." All examples of verbalizing the symptoms but never verbalizing the cause, "I feel so much pain."

When I shared these symptoms with my therapist, she helped me to identify the cause and guided me to releasing the pain in a safe way. As surely as I knew that Dellene could help me through this difficult time, there were times when my fight to block the pain also blocked that awareness. All of my energy went toward trying to keep the pain buried. But once you open that door and begin facing your abuse, there's no stopping the pain associated with it. There were times before or during a session when I'd dig my nails into my palm, hoping the physical pain would stop the emotional pain. Would my therapist see me grasping my palms? Would she ask why? Would she help me? I did not need to leave a mark to elicit help; Dellene understood my emotional state and had the skills to help me find a safe release of my pain. The point is, in my addled mind it was the best I could do to expose my need.

The second reason for self-injury is that inflicting pain becomes a means to feel. In chapter 10, "Depression," I referred to apathy as a state of numbness. When the emotional pain is overbearing, some degree of numbness is a good thing, a means of protection. However, after someone has felt emotionally numb for days or even weeks, the need to feel something—anything—builds, and the state of numbness becomes frightening, leading the person to wonder, *Will I ever feel any emotion again?*

At certain points, I had the thought that physical pain would be better than feeling nothing at all. I wrote the following journal entry during the very devastating weeks when I was facing the realization that Clara had participated in my abuse along with Rune. My response to the emotional pain was to shut down and feel nothing.

August 1, 2008

This is just exactly how it felt: NOTHING.
Little girl feels nothing.
Adolescent girl feels nothing.
Adult woman feels nothing.
NOTHING.
[I bite the side of my hand.]
Okay, I can feel physical pain.
I can feel anger stirring inside.
I can feel hunger.
I can feel tired.
I can feel hot and cold.
Do I want more? Maybe.

The realization that the pain I had buried for a lifetime was about to explode left me terrified. Retreating to a state of numbness offered protection from the pain, but the void frightened me. I needed to feel something. I believed inflicting physical pain would meet that need. Biting my hand did so for a fleeting moment; however, I was left with the same level of emotional pain.

The third reason for self-injury is that physical pain is a means of allowing emotional pain to escape. When it became too difficult for me to face the cause of my emotional pain and impossible to contain it, physical pain became a release. The next journal entry is one example of my contemplating how it would feel to self-injure.

October 25, 2001

I thought again of how good one cut would feel. I could see the anger and pain escape.

There were many times when I'd lie on my bed, door closed, wanting to take a pin and make just one scratch.

Couldn't the pain find its escape through the layers of my skin? Like a slow leak in a tire, seeping out until it was gone. Just one prick and I won't do it again. Just once to see if I can empty this vessel filled with pain.

As illogical as this thought is now, during times of intense emotional pain, the visual image of pain escaping through a cut seemed viable. It would also mean my not having to face the reason for the pain. Pain escaping and escaping pain: neither is a path to healing.

If communicating, feeling, and releasing emotional pain are valid reasons to self-injure, then the next question becomes: Why not turn to self-injury as a response to emotional pain? Because, however it's used, self-injury is a potentially dangerous, unhealthy way to cope with emotional pain. Furthermore, *it does not work*. The internal scars of emotional pain become visibly represented by physical scars, and the victim is victimized once again. The goal isn't just to cope with the pain—the goal is to be healed. Healing will take place only when the source of the pain is addressed and expressed in a safe, healthy manner.

The emotional scars are deep, and the process to healing is long. As new feelings rise to the surface, the urge to self-injure mounts. As I stated earlier, emotional pain doesn't peak and then disappear. The pain ebbs and flows, and you must be ready to brave the storm each time. How, then, throughout this journey, do we brave this storm of pain? How do we stave off the urge to inflict pain?

Think of the strategies as weapons in the fight. If you have a few weapons to draw on when the desire to self-injure is strong, one of them will likely succeed in getting you past that urge. It is only one moment at a time that you need to get past; once the urge is gone, you are safe.

Many of the six strategies that comprised my arsenal of weapons in my personal fight against self-injury are based on mental images and thoughts that I learned from my therapist: ride through the feeling, remember your core, make a promise, you only have to get through this moment. Her words became embedded in my mind, available for the times when I needed them most. As long as your own strategies result in a victory over the urge to inflict physical pain, your options are limitless.

The urge to self-injure is just that—an urge. Emotions build, the alternatives for dealing with the pain narrow, the desire to feel physical pain intensifies. As surely as you believe the emotional pain won't stop, it does. And as it eases, your thoughts become more focused and your desire to self injure fades. If by drawing on one weapon you can fight that urge, you'll ride through the feeling, safe and relieved that you did not give in to a destructive response to pain. I wrote the following journal entry after seeking advice from Dellene on how to cope with my own destructive urges.

December 4, 2001

Dellene helped me understand my feelings. I was able to be very open. I told her I hadn't felt suicidal but felt like hurting myself. Cutting with glass—pretty extreme hurting—to release pain. Again she said usually if you can ride through it, the feeling passes.

For me, riding through the feeling often meant "playing Dellene tapes." *If you give in, you are victimizing yourself over and over again. You've already survived; you can survive this. If you give in, you are giving them the ultimate power. You only have to get through this moment. We will deal with the rest when the time is right.* The following two journal entries illustrate the importance of having Dellene's words to draw on as weapons against self-injury.

February 1, 2004

Over and over I played Dellene tapes in my head: get through this moment, get through this day. And I did.

June 16, 2002

I hate this part. My inner thoughts are the worst. I want to hurt myself. I've learned what it's all about—turning the anger and pain inward—but it's hard to stop it, it's hard not to act on the feeling. What would Dellene say? Fight it, ride it out, because the urge will pass.

Positive thoughts have power over the negative response to inflict pain. It takes effort and concentration, but remember, this fight is designed to keep you from being victimized all over again. It is worth every bit of your strength. Often when I "rode through the feeling," I was left empowered and victorious.

Another weapon against self-injury is to remember your core. I wrote the following journal entry after a session with Dellene to help me to remember *my* core when I was alone and self-destructive thoughts were prevalent.

June 18, 2002

I just got back from my session. I'm beat but there are some things I need to remember. I'm filled, bursting with intense emotion, but I don't let myself think the words that go with the feelings. I feel destructive but fight acting on it. Violence, punching, hurting myself, screaming, crashing my car, going berserk are all what I feel. I'm hanging on by a thread but I'm hanging on. Dellene says it is the core of me that's always been there to get me through.

Throughout your therapy, it will be essential to remember that as broken as you may feel by abuse, there is a core of you that survived. It is that core that remains at the very center of your soul. It got you through the abuse and will get you through the darkness. If you are able to concentrate on your core, you will gain inner strength, a feeling of pride that you made it. That strength will sustain you until the urge to self-injure passes.

As a mother and an educator, I was keenly aware of the image I projected throughout my healing journey. I wanted my children to see me as a strong individual, but exhaustion, stress, and weight loss—all a part of doing the work—made this image of strength hard to maintain. Giving in to self-injury would have made it impossible. At one point of desperation, a time when I fought the urge to use self-injury as my outlet, I had the following startling experience, and used the image as another weapon in my arsenal.

January 13, 2002

Friday at the grocery store, the woman bagging for me had white scars up both arms—several. It was such a shock to me. Oh my God, is that what it would look like? I'd cut and cut again and keep cutting and have scars that people would see? I have to stay so strong against hurting myself.

A stranger, someone who may or may not have caused her own scarring, brought me to a stark reality and gave me strength. Until that day, I had never thought about what I would look like if I acted on my urges. I was horrified at the thought of my children, my students, or anyone else seeing me in the way I saw that woman—with permanent, physical scars representing my emotional pain.

When my pain mounted, I'd re-create the image of that woman in the grocery store. The thought of brandishing those scars on my own body sickened me and was enough to keep me from acting on my urge. Focusing on these visible reminders of self-injury can be a powerful weapon in the fight.

At times, something as simple as making a promise can prevent you from acting on an urge. The following journal entry is really a promise to myself.

December 4, 2001

I told Dellene my strength against hurting myself is not wanting to expose that dark side of myself to anyone.

Whether it is to your therapist, spouse, partner, or friend, making a promise puts both you and the other person on guard. During sessions when I was not at risk, Dellene would tell me that when I did feel like hurting myself, I had to tell her and also tell Tim. I made two promises: I'd tell them when I had the urge to self-injure, and I would not hurt myself. They were the two people who had walked every step of this journey with me. The thought of telling them I had acted on my urge was devastating. They would never have used the word *disappointed*, but I would feel I had disappointed them, let them down. This became a strong weapon for me: I had made a promise, and I'd keep it.

Having come so far in my journey, I can now say the true promise should be to yourself: *I promise I won't hurt myself. I will keep myself safe, because that's what I deserve.*

Keeping in mind that if you can ride through the feeling, it will pass, you may also find that creating a distraction is another important weapon against self-injury. The following journal entry describes a time when creating a distraction kept me safe.

October 28, 2004

I feel pain tonight through to my bones. Ripping at my insides. Pain that feels like knives cutting my insides. Weights hanging off of me. I tell my body to relax but it only lasts a minute. Why does it hurt so bad? What is it? I need to stop writing because I want to bite, scratch, hurt myself to get out the pain. I need to distract myself.

It will sometimes be difficult to create a distraction, but it is possible to do so until the urge to self-injure subsides. Being with another person can be a very effective distraction. It is unlikely that you'll hurt yourself in the company of someone else. If someone is in your home, go to the room they're in. If you live alone, sit outside or go to a public area, such as a library or store. If my husband was home, I'd seek him out, sometimes explaining, sometimes sitting with him in silence until I felt safe.

If it isn't possible to be around others, let the television be a distraction. Although you might not be able to concentrate on a show, the noise and visuals can be enough to get you through the moment. When turning on the television became too great a task for me, I'd simply lie flat on my bed with my hands at my sides, still, quiet, void of thought. That motionless, mindless escape made time pass until either I fell asleep or my urge to self-injure subsided.

The best weapon in the fight against self-injury is sometimes the most difficult: letting someone know the state you are in. Make a phone call to your therapist, a crisis hotline, your spouse, or a friend. Tell them you feel you could hurt yourself. They're there to help. I recommend telling someone as the first strategy you turn to, but I know from my personal experience how difficult that sometimes is. When I contemplated telling someone I wanted to hurt myself, the following thoughts would hold me back: verbalizing the desire would make it more real; it was embarrassing or shameful to admit I wanted to self-injure; telling would be giving up control; if I told, I would then have to deal with the cause of my pain, which was exactly what I was hiding from.

However, pain is real, and you must realize the cause of it in order to become whole. There is no shame in this process; *you* did not cause this pain. Telling someone is not giving up control. It is taking an active step in keeping you safe. The goal is to be whole and healed, and you cannot accomplish that goal alone. Telling someone is not only the safest weapon but also the *surest* weapon in the fight against self-injury.

There were many times throughout my healing journey when I fought the urge to self-injure as a means to communicate, feel, or release emotional pain. By using my arsenal of weapons, I won that fight time and again. Only once, and only for a moment, did I act on the urge. The following journal entry describes the one battle I lost.

December 4, 2005

Feeling empty, I couldn't stand the pain and I took a pin—I needed to see myself bleed, I needed to feel pain. In all of this I have been strong about fighting that part but now I was losing ground. I stuck my thumb three times—deep—watching the blood drip down my hand. I got scared and had enough sense to call Dellene. She walked me through throwing the pin out and telling Tim what I had done. I was so disappointed in myself and embarrassed to have them know.

By calling my therapist after this incident, I was guided back to a safe place and assured that we would deal with my emotional pain in a healthy way.

I expose this experience to say loud and clear that acting on an urge can happen to anyone. Even though I disappointed and embarrassed myself by taking that action, no one was disappointed in me. No one gave up on me. I am so thankful I made that phone call—perhaps a moment too late, but I made it. The memory of the experience became another weapon in my fight against self-injury.

If you prepare your own arsenal of weapons against self-injury, you will be able to take control and keep safe until you can deal with the urge in a healthy, therapeutic setting. With each victory, you will gain added strength and conviction that you are a survivor!

Suicide

Thoughts of suicide—also known as suicidal ideation—are typically an abuse victim's second response to emotional pain. Suicide is an unsettling topic to discuss, and it's one that most people avoid, as no one wants to admit they have entertained such thoughts. However, as grave and uncomfortable as the subject is, it must be addressed. For myself and, I suspect, many other victims, suicidal thoughts are a part of this journey—the darkest part. The uplifting thought is that you can walk through the darkness. Just as there are weapons to help you in the fight against self-injury, there are ways to fight suicidal thoughts until you feel safe or are in the care of a professional.

Prior to sharing my experiences, I must make this crucial statement: if you are having suicidal thoughts, or someone else you know is having them, you *must* tell a trained professional. A therapist is the first person you can reach out to. If you do not have a therapist, call a doctor. If no doctor is available, there are crisis hotlines in every state staffed by trained personnel. Calling 911 is another option. None of the experiences and strategies I will share supersede the importance of getting professional help. My goal here is to offer insight for those who have never experienced hopelessness.

It is impossible to comprehend what goes through the mind of a person considering suicide. We associate hopelessness, desperation, and depression with suicidal thoughts but have little understanding of the feelings behind those words. To an outsider, there's always hope or a better way to cope with despair. It never appears as dark on the outside as it feels on the inside. But how does the darkness seep in? How do one's thoughts turn to such a final escape? The following two journal entries are very telling. My purpose in sharing them is to help others who are walking the journey with a victim gain an understanding of what goes through the mind of someone on the edge of darkness, in an hour of hopelessness. The feelings—hollow, detached, invisible—seem insurmountable. The thought of not going on is a means of escaping the feelings, not an actual intention to die.

January 17, 2005

7:20 AM. Something feels awful. I'm sitting in my living room but I feel detached. I could easily not be here. I need to allow myself to feel this. Invisible, unattached, unknown. If this were the last day of my life, would it matter? What's happening to me? I can't feel any emotional attachment. I can only sit, breathe, stare, and occasionally write a sentence. Hollow. I want to feel but I have no feelings.

I can list the people that it would matter to—Tim Ry Shell Tracee Nancy Dellene Jerry Ellen Gina Chrissy Jake Joyce Deb—but would it really matter? They'd go on.

I can't feel any emotion but I can feel physical pain. If I did not exist, then how did I come to exist?

Empty hollow invisible, a thing an empty body shell, still quiet unheard voiceless feelingless used object.

9:00 AM. I made coffee. Feel a little different, feel like I could slip back. I need to hold on to something, someone today or I'll slip away. I still don't know what I am feeling. Where I was earlier t. is morning is too scary.

Shortly after I wrote this entry, I spoke with Dellene and made a plan to get through that day, by scheduling an appointment with her, having my husband by my side, and staying in the moment.

January 28, 2003

I stopped writing and began to cry. I couldn't stop—I was sobbing. I kept thinking that I don't want to die and the more I thought it, the more I cried. I was finally able to call out to Tim. He was so worried and when I finally said aloud, "I don't want to die," he panicked, insisted we needed help, and called the crisis hotline. The worker asked how she could help, what I felt, then she and Tim worked out reaching Dellene. When Dellene called I mostly cried, shared that I didn't want to die. She assured me that was a good step and just let me cry—"let it go."

Letting it go allowed me to release some of my pain. My tears became the healthy escape I needed. By reaching out, making a call, being guided to address my feelings in a safe manner, I replaced my thoughts of suicide with a small glimmer of hope—the hope I needed to get through the darkness for that moment.

So how does one get through the darkness? As difficult as it is, there are strategies that will help you get past that dark place and into the light. Three of the four possibilities involve other people, because, at your darkest moment, when you want to pull completely into yourself, you have to let someone in. When you feel hopeless, that is the most important time to gain hope and strength from the people you have trusted along this journey.

Medical Intervention

If you are fighting thoughts of suicide, there are two types of medical intervention that you should consider. Again, I am speaking as a survivor, so you should explore these intervention options with a health care professional.

The first option is medication. Many medications are available to help people cope with depression, anxiety, and flooding thoughts—all conditions that could lead to self-injury and suicide. In consultation with my therapist, my health care provider, and a psychiatrist, I accepted medication as a way to help me through the hardest times. It was a difficult decision for me. I needed to be convinced it wouldn't slow my work in therapy or mask the demons I needed to face. I had to view taking medication as a choice, not as giving up control. The medication acted as a buffer, making sleep and everyday life more manageable, while I continued working in therapy.

The second medical option is hospitalization. As I have mentioned, it was not one I favored. Still, at a much earlier session, I had a discussion with Dellene about going to the hospital. The following journal entry describes that conversation.

December 4, 2001

I was comfortable enough to ask specifically what would happen if I did go to the hospital. She went through it step by step. It's something I would not want to experience—more exposure— but it's an option for safety if that's ever what I need.

Although I opposed hospitalization, if it had been what had to happen to keep me safe, I would have accepted that option. If you are at risk and alone, a hospital can provide the safe intervention you need to get you through the moment.

In addition to medical interventions, still other strategies can help get you through the dark times. I call these strategies Beacons of Light because that is what they provided: a lighted path through the darkness. I used them during my darkest moments, as well as at other times throughout my journey. By focusing on my Beacons of Light at less desperate times, I was often able to prevent myself from slipping further into the darkness.

The first time my therapist asked me, "Do you feel suicidal?" I was taken aback. *No one actually asks that*, I thought. In truth, though, the question must be asked, and I needed to accept that and answer it honestly. I wrote the following journal entry after a session with Dellene when I shared that I was losing hope. She asked Tim to come into the room to explain the importance of asking the question.

June 2, 2001

She told Tim that I assured her that I would not hurt myself but that he needs to ask me if I want to hurt myself. The question will not cause the action. I need to be asked.

The key sentence here is: *The question will not cause the action.* Knowing I'd be asked the question put me on guard. I could not hide my thoughts from those who were on this journey with me if they asked directly. I did not want to admit to them that I wasn't safe, but if it was true, I knew they would intervene. This in itself—knowing I'd be asked and knowing I would receive help—gave me hope that I'd make it through the dark times. "Do you feel suicidal?" "Do you want to hurt yourself?" "Are you safe right now?" These questions were Beacons of Light.

The Ultimate Win

In chapter 5, "Journaling," I mentioned writing about insights my therapist shared that became saving graces. They were phrases I could read or replay in my mind to help me through this journey. She often said, "Hurting yourself is giving them the power to hurt you again." I would be giving my abusers the ultimate win. In the following two journal entries, this potent thought gave me the strength I needed to get through that moment.

May 30, 2001

I had thoughts again today of not going on. Where it feels blank beyond me. I thought about having notes written just in case. No—he will not gain the ultimate control.

July 12, 2001

One more thing to remember from my session—I was honest with Dellene about my feelings and fears of desperation. She said I had to share that with Tim. That when I feel like that, he or she or both have to know. Again, it would be the ultimate "win" for Rune.

My abusers had stolen years from me. There was no way I'd allow them to take another second, let alone my life. My anger at the thought of their "winning" rises in me to this day. Focusing on the thought that suicide would be their ultimate win became a powerful Beacon of Light in my fight against suicidal thoughts.

The final strategy against suicidal thoughts has to do with control. As I explained in chapter 7, "Control," there will be times when it will be in your best interest to let others be in control. No time is more important than when you are fighting suicidal thoughts. As much as you dislike giving up control, it may be what prevents you from acting on your thoughts. And ultimately, you *are* still in control, because you are making the sound choice to allow someone else to take control for you, just for the moment. I wrote the following journal entry after one of the times when I made that good choice. I wasn't happy doing so, but on some level I knew it was what I needed.

January 24, 2003

It's been twenty-seven hours of hell. I saw Dellene at five. Had to have Tim pick me up at six, Nancy stay with me until nine, meet Dellene and Tim back at Paddock Crisis at nine fifteen. I bared my soul and sometimes feel like I lost a part of me. Yes, my thoughts

have been dark. I've put lots of thought into ending this. My greatest
fear is that I don't have the strength to go on to face this pain and
that I will give in to death. Yes, I fight it, yes, I know what (who) I
have to live for but I still can feel myself slip down that black hole. I
admitted to Dellene that I held a bottle of pills in my hand—a test.
I said no but will I next time? She suggests we talk to Tim and let
him have control of my meds. It makes me angry but by the end
of that first session and crying in pain and feeling vulnerable and
weak, I agree. So Tim and I will meet with her after nine to discuss
this. I'm drained and don't want to go to this meeting. I don't want
Tim to know how bad it is. We go, Dellene explains—he's tense,
quiet, and I know worried that I'm not okay to go home. She men-
tions the hospital. Fuck that. I'm giving up so much control sharing
my soul—do you really think I'd go to a hospital? So we talk about
him taking my meds—she says even Tylenol, aspirin, ibuprofen. I
hate it. "What do you hate about it?" Dellene asks. We go through
this whole thing for me to admit I need help right now—and I do—
but part of me wants them to leave me alone, part of me wants
them to save me. What do I want? So Tim has all of my meds. The
plan is to talk to Dellene daily for now. To have Tim and Nancy ask
me if I am safe, how I am.

This journal entry illustrates the Beacons of Light that lit my
way through this dark moment. I answered the questions and relin-
quished control. The strategies worked together to provide a safety
net tightly wrapped around me. They allowed me to get past this
moment of despair to a time when I could continue working on the
pain of abuse in a healthy way. As a team, we broke through the darkness just enough for me to believe there was light, life, and hope for
the future. The next journal entry illustrates how that hope became a
buttress when my dark feelings returned.

August 20, 2003

At a session shortly after that last entry I did admit that I was on
the edge, feeling scared, like I could fall into that dark hole. But

I was on the stronger side of that edge. Able to keep from falling. I've been feeling stronger.

Each time you get past a moment of despair, a bit of strength builds. If you can make it through one episode, then you know there's hope that you will make it through again.

Summary

And now we've made it through the darkness, a candid discussion on self-injury and suicide. The journey does get dark, the emotional pain feels insurmountable, and the thoughts of a final escape are real. By creating an arsenal of weapons and Beacons of Light, you can make it through the darkest moments. Remember that you are not alone, and that you cannot do this alone. The weapons to fight self-injury and the Beacons of Light to get you through the darkness will work only if you are dealing with the emotional pain in a healthy manner, with professional help. The pain does not go away—it must work its way out. I have attested to urges to self-injure. I have attested to suicidal thoughts. And finally, with joy, I attest to this fact: as the emotional pain of sexual abuse is released, a bright light shines within! There is a light at the end, and the end is the beginning.

Part IV:
Life

What happens once the scars have been revealed and healed? Life.

In this section, you'll learn about adjusting to the new you, dealing with bumps in the road, and sharing your journey.

12
The Ongoing Journey

Excerpt from Chapter 1, "Setting the Stage"

Her appearance: a good girl, one who liked to please, always willing to help. Her reality: a fragile child, seeking approval, needing to be seen, never feeling good enough. Someone spending a lifetime trying to be "the good daughter."

As a child, eager to do the right thing. As a teen, Clara's confidant during the worst years of Rune's alcoholism. As an adult, taking care of Clara's needs and striving to gain her attention and approval. All the while never feeling as smart, good, pretty, or well liked as her peers. I secretly doubted most of my decisions and always fell short of feeling accomplished or whole.

That little girl and woman will never be forgotten. They are my past. Facing my demons, reliving my memories, and releasing the resulting emotions have left me cleansed of my years of abuse. My scars are healed. To say I feel whole hardly describes the person who has evolved on this journey. I live in the present, no longer waiting for the next shoe to drop. I celebrate my strengths and know my weaknesses. I know I am equal to, not less than, my peers. I appreciate the joy in my life and trust that I deserve to feel that joy. And the greatest revelation: I believe I am loved.

In this final chapter, I'll talk about the ongoing journey, because life is just that. Healing the scars of abuse allows you to emerge as a new person, or, as I prefer to think, evolve into the person you were meant to be. A part of this ongoing journey is adjusting to the new you. Feelings of self-confidence, joy, love, and trust will seem foreign to you at first, but I'll discuss strategies for adjusting until the new you becomes the norm.

Situations throughout your life may trigger old fears or feelings. I'll also share my experiences and how to manage what I call the bumps in the road. For some survivors, there are leftover issues that they never faced; I'll show you that you are equipped to conquer that mountain. Finally, I'll talk about the ripple effect of sharing your journey with others.

Adjusting to the New You

Whether you are a survivor of rape or childhood sexual abuse, the experience will cause changes in your behavior and self-perception. Depression and anxiety affect both how you view the world and how you relate to others; healing the scars of abuse will help change those negative perceptions. If you are an adult victim of rape, you will eventually reclaim the person you were before the abuse. If you were sexually abused as a child, you grew up not knowing who you really are, as your self-esteem diminished beginning with the first sexual act. As you face your abuse and heal, you'll be able to evolve into the person you were meant to be.

It is important to understand that all of this is a process. Some days you will feel strong, confident, and well adjusted. Other days you may awake insecure or unhappy with yourself. All it takes is a kind or disparaging word to make the difference in how you feel.

Here's the part that's especially hard to comprehend: feeling good about yourself, your relationships, and life has not been the norm. You may question what your newfound confidence is. It is difficult to break old patterns of self-doubt. The following journal entry expresses how scary it was to believe in myself.

July 31, 2003

For the first time ever, I'm beginning to feel I have a real relation-
ship with Tim. I trust that he loves me. I know I love him. I am
not thinking about what I "should" say, do, feel, with him. We
just are. For days I was so unsettled, confused, even depressed.
It took Dellene to help me sort it out. This is a first for me. What
I'm accustomed to is feeling criticism, never quite measuring up,
always trying to please, never believing I was "pleasing" by being
me. This new feeling is out of my comfort zone, it's making me
emotional, it's scary and wonderful all at once. Dellene helped
me see that I need to relax and enjoy and get used to the piece of
me that is healing and let the rest come.

The key to what Dellene told me is to enjoy and get used to the
"piece" of me that is healing. Confidence comes in stages and takes
time. When the good feelings are present, don't question them.
Simply acknowledge that they are real. They will soon become the
most prevalent feelings you have.

Now that I am a much more confident person, I do not question
all of my words or actions, nor do I think others are always judging
me. That is not to say there aren't times when I waver. If someone
says something nice about me, I sometimes wonder if it's for their
own gain, rather than a sincere compliment. I still have moments
when my first reaction is to doubt myself if someone disagrees with
me. When the self-doubt returns and you find yourself listening to
old tapes in your head, awareness is key.

Be aware of how you react to situations when you are feeling
good about yourself, versus being hard on yourself. You'll see that
your thoughts are clearly different. When you are in a situation in
which you doubt yourself, you need a reminder that that's the old you
reacting. You can accomplish this level of awareness by making it an
exercise in your journal. In a quiet moment, visualize your mood,
posture, and inner thoughts when your self-esteem is low. Write
it all down. Do the same thing again, this time citing examples of
moments when you were confident.

By creating this awareness, you will have something to draw on when you are feeling low. Once you are aware it is the "old you" reacting, you can try to adjust. Remind yourself that you've done the work to heal. You are a survivor and thriver, no longer a victim. This idea will help you regain confidence.

Self-talk, along with journal writing, is another great tool for maintaining awareness of your confidence. Deciding my husband thinks I'm a bad person because I left our car's gas tank empty is a whole lot different than realizing he is simply not happy I left the car that way—and who *would* be happy about that? In the first scenario, I view myself as a "bad" person for leaving the gas tank empty. In the second scenario, I accept responsibility for doing so without turning it into a lack of self-worth. Without the awareness of where that first feeling came from, the old me, I'd dwell on negative thoughts.

A final strategy for adjusting to the new you is to celebrate! Don't be afraid of the person you've become. Celebrate your confidence, your ability to feel loved, your new awareness that you are a person with strengths, weaknesses, good traits, and traits that still need work. Think about it, write it in your journal, read it when you are feeling less worthy, and share those positive thoughts with the people you trust. And, greatest of all, be proud—proud that you faced your demons and did the work to heal. You did not let your abuser ruin you. You rose above the demeaning blows they dealt you and emerged a better person. Celebrate the blossoming, new you.

> *And the time came when the risk to remain tight in a bud*
> *was more painful than the risk it took to blossom.*
> —Anaïs Nin

Bumps in the Road

Months, even years, go by. You are living your life as a survivor, healed and whole. Life is good—until something happens that nudges you back in time or slams you against a wall. You feel as though you are back in the depths, facing your abuse, anxious, angry, sad. You don't know how to react, if you will recover, or if joy will ever return to your life. The following journal entry explores Dellene's explanation for why there are temporary setbacks in the journey.

January 8, 2005

Over vacation I felt a way I've never felt—strong, comfortable, at peace with myself, not driven, not anxious. I was in a place I want to be in forever. As vacation went on and work returned, that feeling passed. I was back to my old self and it upset me. I called Dellene. She said I had been through years of abuse and years of feeling one way about myself. That even though I had a taste of letting go of the old ideas, it was the easiest thing to slip back into. But it doesn't mean I won't get back to the "good place." I will, and each time it will last longer. I need to be patient.

When you are in that "good place" for long periods of time, there will still be bumps in the road. Their cause and severity will vary. They can be related to the time of year, a news story that brings back memories, seeing someone from your past, a loss in your life, or even something that has no obvious explanation. Whatever the cause, it creates a resurgence of the anxiety, anger, or sadness you experienced related to your abuse. I've had my share of these bumps in the road—as all survivors of sexual abuse have, I'm sure. We have experienced trauma. We have healed the scars, but they're still a part of who we are. We can't erase our past. So how can we cope with a bump in the road? By employing two simple strategies.

First, remember that a bump is only a bump. Even if it sets you back to being anxious, angry, or sad, you will never revert to where you were at the beginning of this journey. Initially, hitting a bump scared me; I thought all the progress I had made was lost, and I felt as if I would never be at peace again. But with the help of my therapist, I learned to recognize these setbacks as temporary—and you will, too. You've learned coping strategies, you have an understanding of who you are, you believe in yourself, and you know *you* did not cause your abuse. All the good you've done to heal will propel you over that bump. It may take an hour, a day, a week, or longer, but you will return to feeling whole. I know, because I've been there.

Another common reaction when something sets you back is to ignore the feeling or try to push it aside. You are doing well and want to hide from anything that could change that. However, hiding will not make it go away. What *will* help you get past a setback is talking about it. If you are still seeing your therapist, discuss it at your next session. If you've stopped having regular appointments, try to make contact. Sometimes one or two visits or phone calls are enough. If your therapist is unavailable, talk with someone who has traveled the journey with you. Saying out loud that you are anxious, angry, or sad will help you sort through what's causing those feelings. Talking it out and identifying the cause might be all you need to get back on track. In the following journal entry, I couldn't identify what was upsetting me until I talked it over with Dellene.

March 17, 2004

Recently I was sickened by thoughts of Rune, even feeling anxious, like something new was coming. But then Dellene asked if there was anything significant about the time of year. Of course—March 13 he died. I'm feeling better again. It's passed. The good part here is that I've learned to believe that he is dead, gone—he can never hurt, sicken, or scare me again.

When something brought back disturbing thoughts of my abuser, Dellene helped me to identify that it related to the date when he died. By talking about it, I was able to reassure myself of all the good things I learned in therapy—namely, that he could never hurt me again.

Conquering a Mountain

Some bumps will feel more like mountains. They may be caused by a memory that didn't surface in the past or by an unexpected encounter with someone associated with your abuse. The uncomfortable feelings start bubbling up and become impossible to suppress. This is a sign that something needs to be identified and addressed. It is up to you to take control and seek help—again, if at all possible, with your therapist, although you can also work through the situation with a loved one. The potential need for a more involved intervention also exists in this kind of scenario.

I spent years in therapy talking about Clara's knowledge of my abuse and her choice not to protect me. Session after session revolved around my being able to accept and let go of the fact that I did not have a mother in the true sense of the word. Months after I ended my relationship with Clara, my healing journey seemed complete. I no longer saw my therapist on a regular basis, though we kept in touch over the phone. Life was going along smoothly. I made the decision to retire from my teaching job to spend time with my husband and work on my book.

Then, in July 2008, I found myself standing at the base of that mountain.

As resistant as I was to facing this final obstacle, I drew on the strategies ingrained in me from my years in therapy—trust and open communication with a therapist, communicating information, creating a tear, planned release, and remembering my core—to conquer my mountain.

July 13, 2008

Another piece. I asked how could there be more but deep down I knew there was some unfinished business. It came to the surface through my writing. First I think it is the subject matter but the anxiety builds. That's different—that's my signal that something needs to get out.

Frightened and confused, I knew I had to call Dellene and try to figure this out. Through our phone conversation, I realized my anxiety had to do with Clara. I had never finished the work of knowing deep down that she'd had an active role in my abuse.

July 13, 2008

I always said "she was there" but went no further. Couldn't do it!

I still didn't think I could face what was coming, but my level of anxiety left me with no other choice. When memories are right there on the surface, you cannot and should not try to push them away. I met with Dellene for a few sessions. This was by far the most difficult memory for me to confront. I fought hard to stop the thoughts.

July 13, 2008

I don't want to do this—I don't want to believe this. It was the same old fight—I tried as long as I could to stop the thoughts. Then I remembered. Clara prepared me, dressed me in a night-gown, and stood by the door when he came in.

By my next session with Dellene, I knew I was fighting something even greater. One horrid memory remained buried but was fighting its way to the surface: the ultimate trauma to a young girl's body. Terrified to face this truth, I did something I had never done before: in a session with Dellene, I shut down and refused to speak.

July 17, 2008

I was a mess, very anxious. I knew I had to explore the bathroom soon. Tried but couldn't and shut down. Done—not talking. I figured out if I stayed still and didn't talk, I could be okay.

Tim picked me up, and Dellene explained to him that I was not ready to remember anything more. It took unprecedented trust to build a steel barrier around myself in the presence of the two people who cared the most about my well-being. I remained silent on the drive home, and when we arrived, I got in bed, refusing to eat or speak. The next two journal entries illustrate the importance of communicating information, even if that communication takes on an unconventional form.

July 17, 2008

The next twenty-four hours were hell.

Tim and Dellene stayed in close contact as I lay in an emotionless state. Finally, the next morning, I agreed to communicate through drawings. Tim handed me a pad and pen.

July 17, 2008

I drew graphic pictures of what happened to me in that bathroom. Drew a pic of me now with all the feelings locked in a box inside of me. Wrote, "Where's the key?"

I had locked the fear and pain inside me, and I believed I had no survivable means of expelling these intense emotions. Tim, overcome with worry, called Dellene, telling her about the pictures. She came to the house. Still not speaking, I handed her my pictures.

After looking at the pictures and reading my words—*Where's the key?*—Dellene knew just what to say.

July 17, 2008

Dellene said I was the only one who had the key. That made me cry. Then it just started. I cried and yelled and scraped it all out.

In the safety of my home, with my therapist by my side, I unlocked the emotions, releasing the memory, fear, and pain. I scraped my insides out, finally cleansing myself of this horrific truth.

It took weeks of resting, being cared for, and talking with Dellene and Tim for me to regain my strength and recover, but I did. I hit the base of my mountain, shut down, and, with support, love, and guidance from Tim and Dellene, conquered the worst of my memories. If I had not had that core strength and the belief that I was worth it, and if I had not put in years of hard work in therapy, the outcome of hitting this mountain could have been quite different. But I propelled myself over it and prevailed!

Sharing Your Journey

You've spent years in therapy, exposing and healing the most horrific scars of sexual abuse. You are healed and experiencing joy. Your life is moving forward, and you are in it, in the present. Your past is just that—behind you.

So why would anyone want to talk about the past? Share that journey? Rehash the most difficult years of their life? Because doing so creates a positive ripple effect. By sharing your story of abuse and healing, you might open the door for someone else to break their silence. You are now living proof that there is hope for other survivors. Without even knowing it, you're lending others courage—the courage it takes to heal.

Talking about your past is not easy, but once you witness this ripple effect of sharing hope and courage, you'll look forward to any opportunity you have to reveal your journey. The following three examples give testimony to the joy I experienced once I became open about mine.

A Gift Received

Initially, I was cautious about—and perhaps even afraid of—telling my story. Would people believe me? Would it make others uncomfortable? How would I even begin the conversation? But then it just happened unexpectedly. Now, the memory is one that I enjoy retelling.

Still working as a teacher, I had just started writing this book. I realized I'd need a reader along the way to provide feedback on my writing. One of my colleagues, with whom I had worked for years, not only taught her students how to write but also instilled in them a love for writing. I knew she'd be the perfect person to give me input, but she did not know anything about my abuse.

I stopped her one day and said, "I'm writing a book, and I'm wondering if you would be willing to read it and provide feedback."

She seemed a bit surprised, but she agreed.

As I walked away, my heart landed somewhere in my stomach. *Oh*

205205205205

my gosh—if she's going to read the book, I'm going to have to tell her what it's about! I never considered that!

It sounds absurd, but it never dawned on me that the person reading my writing would be exposed to my story. That night, I printed the first two chapters, put them in an envelope, and attached a note explaining why I was writing this book. I left it on her desk at the end of the next day.

In the morning, I found a sealed note on my desk. The letter expressed a heartfelt and personal message opening the door to more conversations about the prevalence of sexual abuse. Soon after that, we met to discuss the initial chapters I had shared with her. It was the beginning of a friendship that has since turned into a very special relationship. A naive request to read my story blessed me with a person who I believe was put in my life to fill the void left when I disconnected from my biological family. Sharing my story brought me that gift.

Lending Courage

As time went on, I became more comfortable with telling others about my abuse. It often happened when someone asked, "What do you do?" and I responded, "I'm writing a book."

"What are you writing about?"

"I'm writing an inspirational book for survivors of sexual abuse, because that is my story."

That very conversation has happened too many times for me to remember. The response has been the same almost every time: "I/my sister/my friend/my spouse/my daughter/my mother was abused, too."

Sadly, most victims of abuse haven't gone through therapy to address their experience. In some cases, I was the first person they'd even told about it. In the conversation that followed those first few questions, I let them know they, or their loved one, are not alone and that there is hope that they, too, can get the help they need to heal. Many of these people have stayed in touch with me through e-mails and phone calls. Some have started therapy. By sharing my story, I became tangible proof that healing is possible.

Creating a Bond

I'm going to end with a compelling example of the ripple effect of sharing my story of abuse. It is deeply personal and has left an indelible impression on my life. With her permission, I will share the story of my Aunt Grethe.

Aunt Grethe is Rune's younger sister. Our families spent holidays and went on summer picnics together throughout my youth. When I became an adult, Clara began telling me stories of Aunt Grethe. They all centered on the "fact" that Aunt Grethe didn't like me or my husband and never asked about my children. Of course, at the time I believed Clara. In April 2002, my uncle, Aunt Grethe's husband, died. During that time, Aunt Grethe discovered what I was going through, but we never spoke.

In 2005, I was ready to talk with Aunt Grethe face-to-face, to tell her about Rune and Clara myself, and to share that Clara had told me Aunt Grethe had never liked me. We met for lunch. I can still see the disbelief in her face as she responded. None of what Clara had said was true. Aunt Grethe had never expressed dislike for me or my family; I was her niece; she loved me and always had. She told me she had no doubt of Rune's capacity for abuse. As a mother of two girls, she could not imagine Clara's not protecting me.

That day was the beginning of a new relationship with my aunt. We spoke on the phone and enjoyed visits. She was supportive and tried more than once to persuade Clara to tell the truth.

Aunt Grethe's support and presence in my life were a wonderful result of my having shared my story, but it didn't end there. In March 2007, my cousin told me Aunt Grethe wanted to see me. She had something to tell me. I never imagined what she was about to reveal as I sat at her dining room table. The following journal entry is an excerpt of our heartrending conversation.

March 11, 2007

We sat down and she said, "You are not the only one he abused. When I was a young girl, he abused me. I never told anyone until now." We both cried. How ironic, this person who I thought hated me, now so bonded, victims of the same scum. I felt so connected to her. I thanked her over and again for telling me.

That moment is etched in my heart. We had an indescribable bond now. After we talked, Aunt Grethe finally understood that she was not at fault, and a burden lifted from her—her shame and guilt were gone. A year after Aunt Grethe knew Rune had abused me, she told her daughters what he had done to her. It was the first time in over seventy years that she told anyone she had been sexually abused.

From that day on, Aunt Grethe and I have shared a closeness that no one else could ever fully understand. This woman who I once believed hated me now ends every one of our conversations with "I love you now and always have." The ripple effect of telling her my story has become a blessing for both of us.

Share your own triumph over abuse. Tell your story where and when you can. You never know the lives you will touch, the courage you will lend, the hope you will instill in others who need hope.

Summary

None of us knows what our ongoing journey has in store for us, but, as survivors of sexual abuse, we can be sure the journey will have an imprint from our past. It is the work we do to heal that makes that a blessing and not a curse.

I look at life in a whole new way now. I know I survived for a reason, and I thrive by sharing my story and helping others along the way. As difficult as the healing journey is, its rewards are great. Using strategies to cope, being aware of your feelings, and, most of all, learning to love yourself can transform a life of darkness into a life of joy.

"Just when the caterpillar thought the world was over, it became a butterfly . . ."

Don't be afraid to take the journey. Reveal and heal your scars of abuse. From the dismal cocoon of a victim, you will emerge a beautiful butterfly.

Spread your wings and soar, feel joy, and share the good news.

Acknowledgments

It is with a grateful heart that I acknowledge those who have helped to make this book a reality.

To Kathryn Orzech, who gave of her time to read *Say It Out Loud* in its rougher stages while completing her own novel: thank you for working through the organizational kinks and listening to my groans and glee every step of the way.

To Karen Zordan, my colleague, first reader, and dear friend: thank you for always reminding me that every setback and every forward movement happened for a reason. When I doubted this book would get published, you were my constant ray of hope.

To Annie Tucker, my editor extraordinaire: thank you for editing with such a keen eye and such a warm heart. Your sensitive approach and encouraging words allowed me to take *Say It Out Loud* to the next level. And I say with a big smile, thank you for letting me keep *most* of the punctuation out of my journal entries.

To Nancy McGraw, my dear friend and confidant: thank you for being by my side through some of the most difficult stages of this journey. I will always proudly walk arm in arm with you down any street.

A special thank you to my children, Tracee, Ryan, and Shelly. There was a time when I harbored guilt for the many occasions throughout my journey when I felt I was emotionally unavailable to you. My hope was that in the end you would see that with the love and support of family and friends, you can make it through any adversity you face in life. You have each, in your own way, told me that my journey is an inspiration for you—the greatest gift I could ever hope for.

And to Tim and Dellene: there are no words to thank you, except to say I am here because of you.

Questions for Discussion

1. In *Say It Out Loud,* Roberta discusses examples of using a respite, journaling, and visualization as strategies in her healing journey. Do you feel these same strategies could be used to cope with other challenges? How could you apply them to your life?

2. Roberta learned through trial and error that physical outlets, such as running and racquetball, were more effective for her than verbal expressions when she wanted to release anger. What are some healthy ways you express anger?

3. Roberta repressed her memories of abuse until she was in her forties. Is that difficult for you to comprehend? Why or why not?

4. You learn from this book the importance of balancing control. Are you a person who always has to be in control? If so, what purpose does that serve in your life? What would it mean to cede control to someone or something else?

5. Have you ever found yourself in a position where you had to set boundaries? If so, was that comfortable or uncomfortable for you? How did you establish and assert those boundaries?

6. Roberta struggled with the decision to terminate relationships in her life that were detrimental to her healing. Do you feel you could make that decision? Why or why not?

7. After reading *Say It Out Loud*, do you feel you would be able to support someone dealing with issues of sexual abuse? What are some of the techniques you would employ?

8. In the chapter "Through the Darkness," Roberta candidly discusses thoughts of self-injury and suicide. Have you ever been concerned that a loved one had those same thoughts? Knowing the positive effect it had on Roberta, would you be able to ask the question, "Do you feel like hurting yourself?"

9. Roberta states in her book that her reason for sharing her story is to offer hope to other survivors. Did you feel hopeful after reading *Say It Out Loud?* Why or why not?

10. Is there something you would like to "say out loud"? Are you more willing to now knowing that for Roberta, saying it out loud led her on a journey to healing and wholeness?

About the Author

© Abigail Scott Photography

As a survivor of childhood sexual abuse, Roberta Dolan has made it her mission to enlighten others about the importance of ending the silence and of the need for tangible strategies to support healing. Roberta is a former special-education teacher with a master's degree in counseling. The desire to educate remains at her core as she conducts seminars for parents and childcare providers on preventing childhood sexual abuse.

Say It Out Loud: Revealing and Healing the Scars of Sexual Abuse is Roberta's first book. Her personal story of hope for all victims has been published in RAINN's online journal, *End the Silence*. In an effort to support other new writers, Roberta founded the Writers' Network of Central Connecticut.

When they are not at home in Connecticut, Roberta and her

husband, Tim, enjoy traveling the country in their RV. You can learn more about Roberta on her website, RobertaDolan.com, and her blog, Write-to-Survive.blogspot.com, or follow her on Facebook at Say It Out Loud: Revealing and Healing the Scars of Sexual Abuse and on Twitter: @writetosurvive.

SELECTED TITLES FROM SHE WRITES PRESS

*She Writes Press is an independent publishing company
founded to serve women writers everywhere.
Visit us at www.shewritespress.com.*

*Don't Call Me Mother: A Daughter's Journey from Abandonment to
Forgiveness* by Linda Joy Myers $16.95, 978-1-938314-02-5
Linda Joy Myers's story of how she transcended the prisons of her
childhood by seeking—and offering—forgiveness for her family's sins.

*Letting Go into Perfect Love: Discovering the Extraordinary After
Abuse* by Gwendolyn M. Plano $16.95, 978-1-938314-74-2
After staying in an abusive marriage for twenty-five years, Gwen Plano
finally broke free—and started down the long road toward healing.

A Leg to Stand On: An Amputee's Walk into Motherhood
by Colleen Haggerty $16.95, 978-1-63152-923-8
Haggerty's candid story of how she overcame the pain of losing a leg at
seventeen—and of terminating two pregnancies as a young woman—
and went on to become a mother, despite her fears.

Seeing Red: A Woman's Quest for Truth, Power, and the Sacred
by Lone Morch $16.95, 978-1-938314-12-4
One woman's journey over inner and outer mountains—a quest that
takes her to the holy Mt. Kailas in Tibet, through a seven-year marriage,
and into the arms of the fierce goddess Kali, where she discovers her
powerful, feminine self.

Think Better. Live Better. 5 Steps to Create the Life You Deserve
by Francine Huss $16.95, 978-1-938314-66-7
With the help of this guide, readers will learn to cultivate more creative
thoughts, realign their mindset, and gain a new perspective on life.

The Complete Enneagram: 27 Paths to Greater Self-Knowledge
by Beatrice Chestnut, PhD $24.95, 978-1-938314-54-4
A comprehensive handbook on using the Enneagram to do the self-
work required to reach a higher stage of personal development.